# CONFESSIONS OF A CITY GIRL

# CONFESSIONS OF A CITY GIRL

Suzana S.

Published by Virgin Books 2009

2 4 6 8 10 9 7 5 3 1

This book is substantially a work of non-fiction based on the life, experiences and
recollections of one *Citygirl*, an accurate representation of life in the City of London
during the 2007–2009 global financial crisis, and the realistic challenges that females in
the City may encounter. However, the names of people and companies, places, dates,
sequences or the detail of events have been changed to protect their privacy, and most of
the people mentioned are composites of the many characters the author met in the
course of her City life and not representations of actual persons.

First published in Great Britain in 2009 by
Virgin Books
Random House, 20 Vauxhall Bridge Road,
London SW1V 2SA

www.virginbooks.com
www.rbooks.co.uk

Addresses for companies within The Random House Group Limited can be found at:
www.randomhouse.co.uk/offices.htm

The Random House Group Limited Reg. No. 954009

A CIP catalogue record for this book
is available from the British Library

Trade paperback ISBN 9780753519769

The Random House Group Limited supports The Forest Stewardship Council [FSC],
the leading international forest certification organisation. All our titles that are printed on
Greenpeace-approved FSC-certified paper carry the FSC logo.
Our paper procurement policy can be found at www.rbooks.co.uk/environment

**Mixed Sources**
Product group from well-managed
forests and other controlled sources
www.fsc.org  Cert no. TT-COC-2139
© 1996 Forest Stewardship Council

Printed and bound in Great Britain by
Clays Ltd, St Ives plc

To my grandmother,
Charlotte: a country girl with City smarts.

# Prologue

I TOOK MY SEAT in a plush strip club ten minutes by taxi from the Bank of England. This place was on the northern edge of the 'Viagra triangle' situated in between the tube stations Bank, St Paul's and Liverpool Street. It was noisy, crowded, and full of men. Exactly like my office, funnily enough.

'Come on, lads, let's have another bottle.'

My five colleagues were dropping some serious cash, as were the two clients we'd been entertaining all night. These were the boom days of late 2006 and it was just another Tuesday night out on the town for the City Boys – and for me, the one City Girl who was always in their midst.

One of the hostesses came over with our order. We were drinking champagne. We always seemed to be drinking champagne back then, and always bought the best.

'Not for me, I'm only going to stay another ten minutes.'

'You always do that. Come on, let your hair down. Stay till the end for once. See what we really get up to when the lights go down.'

'If I saw that I'd have to tell your mother on you, Gordon. Or your wife. You don't want me to do that, do you?'

'You're a spoilsport. I knew we should never have got a woman on the floor. Didn't I say we should never get a woman on the team?' He looked at the others then turned and gave me one of his biggest smiles and a classic Gordon wink. Irritating, really, but he was one of my favourites. If there was ever a showdown in the office he'd defend me. He'd insult me, he'd say something hideously sexist and very probably actionable, but in the end he would defend me. Friends like that were hard to find in the City.

Friendship was the real reason I was out with the boys yet again. The truth is that if I didn't end an evening with the guys, I'd be on my own. Last year I'd joined the firm's trainee programme alongside one girl and eighteen wannabe City Boys. The other girl had left after two months. That left me just a bit outnumbered. I traded better than the boys, and made more money than them in the office, but I never got my way in the evenings. One girl wants to go to a jazz club. Eighteen boys fancy the strip club. Do the maths.

'Sure you don't want us to get someone to dance for you, babe? You'd make an old man very happy.'

'Control yourself, Gord. You're not an old man, you just look like one. Now, be a good boy and watch the show.'

The music had picked up and a new set of girls hit the

stage. If you like that sort of thing then the girls were as hot as hell. They were also the most amazing dancers. My colleagues certainly seemed to approve. Even Gordon shut up for a while. I leaned back into my leather sofa and looked around the bar. I wondered idly what my grandmother would think of the place. Curiously, I had a feeling she might approve. I don't know what goes on behind the scenes but on the floor, at least, the women were in total control. They were so good at what they did, they mesmerised the men. It was good to see the girls in charge for a change.

I looked at my watch as the music blared loudly. It was nearly eleven. I needed to be on the 6 a.m. Tube tomorrow morning. I'd be trading at seven and I wanted to do well. It was time to go.

'One more glass?' Another colleague was leaning across, ready to top up my drink. Chivalry wasn't dead, even in this dodgy little East End basement.

'Thanks, guys, but I really am going to go. And, as usual, please don't get up. Not right now.'

I eased my way through the maze of tables towards the stairs. I flagged down a taxi in the street. The club I'd just left was pretty much the only late-night establishment around so the cab driver must have known where I'd come from.

'Interesting night, love?' he asked. I could only see the back of his head but I could tell he was smiling.

'Fascinating, thank you.'

'You work in the City?'

'How could you tell?'

'Your clothes. And the fact that you're leaving a lap-dance club on your own. Funny old world, isn't it?' We talked about how funny it was for the rest of the journey. Towards the end, he asked about my job and wanted to know what life was really like inside Canary Wharf.

'It's not exactly normal,' was my four-word verdict on City life. I was glad we were close to my home at that point. I didn't feel ready to be specific, especially with a taxi driver and especially after the day I'd just had. It had begun with some typically ugly, early morning scenes up on the trading floor. One of the risk managers from our back office had been called in to talk to us about some of the warning signs he had seen in the market. Part of his job was to check every trade we all did – and to pick up the pieces if we got things badly wrong. He saw the bigger picture and could sense market trends before anyone else. But because he talked about risk everyone wanted to ignore him. Traders hated being lectured about risk. They also hated being addressed by someone from within their own firm. The only people City traders respect are the ones parachuted in from a rival bank. Pay your dues in your own company and you're dismissed as a plodder. Try and work your way up the ranks and you're treated with suspicion. I'd made it from administration in the back office right up to the trading floor – and that set me apart from my colleagues far more than being the only girl in the gang. The boys thought I might know where some of their skeletons were buried. So it took me a long time to win their trust. Past experience in other roles counted against you in the City, in 2006. Everything and everyone was supposed to be shiny and new. Anyone who'd stuck around in the same job or wanted to suggest that the good times wouldn't last for ever was ignored, humiliated or pushed back into the sidelines. That morning our risk manager had been heckled from the start. He wanted to warn us that the figures on some trades no longer added up. He tried to say the deals were getting dangerously risky. He got shot down and humiliated at every turn. Someone once said that a trading floor is a cross between a boys' public school and a street gang. It had felt that way today. No one actually spoke out against what the risk manager had said. They just ignored it and mocked the way he said it. After enduring about ten minutes of heckling and jokes he left the floor. Then everyone carried on trading as if he'd never even existed.

I don't think I could have explained all that to my taxi driver even if I'd had the time. But I would have been ready if he'd asked me the next obvious question: why the hell I wanted to be part of that world in the first place. 'Because if you want excitement then nothing else comes close,' I'd have said. The City is a mad world, staffed largely by mad men. Getting in is as tough as hell. Surviving the training, passing the exams and doing the job is no picnic either. But if you make it, and if you beat the boys at their own games, then it's worth it.

'See you another time, love,' my taxi driver said before he drove off. I smiled, because there probably would be another time. A few dodgy nights out with the boys were the easy part of City life. It was the rest of it that could leave you so stressed you could barely speak, so tired you could barely walk. Here's how it was for me.

# Chapter 1

On MY FIRST DAY as a City Girl, I walked into the middle of a mid-summer storm. The sun was shining when I left my flat and headed for the Tube. By the time I got to London Bridge station, the heavens had opened. Rain was pouring down and I didn't know what to do. I'd been up since 6 a.m. getting ready. I'd stuffed my bag with absolutely everything I thought I might need at the office. I'd even bought a copy of the *Financial Times*, although I hadn't actually got as far as reading it. The one thing I didn't have was an umbrella.

'Just get out of the bleeding way!' A smart, middle-aged woman practically spat the words out at me as I hovered at the Tube exit. I suddenly realised that the people rushing past me hadn't been swearing at the weather. They'd been swearing at me. I'd only been in London for a week and I didn't realise how dangerous it was to stand in the way of City commuters. I ran out and tried to find shelter in a shop doorway. But most of the space was taken up by a young guy handing out free newspapers. He didn't look very pleased to see me either. I took a deep breath. I'd just have to go for it.

A mass of dark-clothed, pinstriped clones were headed north towards the City. I joined them. Everyone else had their umbrellas up and they funnelled even more rain on to my shoulders as we waited at the first set of traffic lights. By the time the green man appeared I was soaked – and things got worse in the middle of London Bridge. The rain there was almost horizontal. It's July, I thought, how can the weather be like this? I had been trying to protect my hair with my *FT*, but I very nearly lost my grip on it when a gust of wind took my breath away. I stuffed it back under my arm, suddenly worried that some of the newsprint was running down my face.

The only good news was that my new office was just over the bridge. I threw myself against the glass door just as I saw the sign saying 'pull'. I regrouped and did just that. A man nearly took my eye out as he snapped down his umbrella and strode through the door I'd just opened. He didn't seem to notice me, let alone feel the need to say thanks.

I tried to shake myself down as I walked over to the security desk. 'I'm here for my internship,' I said to the man behind it.

'You look as if you're here to do the front crawl,' the guard said laughing away at his little joke as he passed me the visitors' book. He must have been almost sixty and had a pair of brown thick-rimmed glasses perched on the largest cauliflower nose I'd ever seen. It was covered in purple veins and I couldn't take my eyes off it. 'You'll be wanting Human

Resources. Take a seat and someone will be down in a few minutes.'

I sat on a modern and desperately uncomfortable black leather chair a few feet from the security guard. 'I'd offer you a towel if I had one, but I'm afraid I don't,' he said.

'I'll be fine, thanks,' I said, trying to smile and look away from his nose. Suddenly it was really important to me that this man liked me. I was twenty-three, I'd only just arrived in London from America and I desperately wanted a friend.

Oh my God. There's steam coming off my jacket. I'd been trying to get comfortable for a few moments when I realised I had created my own little eco-system. I looked up to the security desk to try and attract my new friend's attention. 'Is there a Ladies I could use to try and dry myself out a bit before they come to get me?' I asked.

But at that moment a lady from Human Resources arrived. I stood up, hideously aware that I'd left a little puddle behind me on the leather chair. 'I got caught in the rain,' I said, as if she might not have spotted it on her own.

'Don't you just love the British summer?' she said, clicking me through the security gates.

My new companion was about thirty. At about five-eight she was fair bit taller than me and had her hair held back from her face with a shiny blue clip. She was wearing a pair of those glasses that don't have rims and her whole look was busy and businesslike. 'I thought we should get the paperwork out of the way first with one of my colleagues, then you can have a tour of the building and we'll take you to meet the girl you're replacing,' she said as we waited in front of a row of lifts.

When the doors opened, about half a dozen people swarmed in and I was too embarrassed to ask if I could go to the Ladies before starting the paperwork. We stood in silence as the floors added up and the lift gradually emptied. Human Resources clearly had a prime position up in the gods.

'This way. I'm Fiona, by the way, and I'll be handing you over to Sarah for the next half hour or so,' she said. Her pass opened up another set of opaque glass security doors and we headed down a long beige corridor. We walked into small room with a very big view. Floor-to-ceiling windows overlooked the River Thames. I couldn't fail to notice that the rain had stopped and the sun had come out again. I could hardly have timed my first-ever commute worse.

Sarah, who stood as we arrived, looked almost identical to Fiona. Same age, same height, pretty much the same hair and same thin, rimless glasses. Am I the only person who wears contact lenses, I asked myself as I shook her hand. 'I got caught in the rain,' was my opening gambit for the second time. I caught Sarah's quick glance out of the window. The sun was now intense. I desperately wanted to go back to bed and start the whole day again tomorrow.

'We need to fill in some forms to get you a security pass, and get you access to the right systems here. I need to tell you some things about the building and our emergency procedures. Feel free to interrupt and ask questions,' Sarah said, sitting down again and opening a file.

'Could I put this in a bin, please?' I asked, holding up my still sodden newspaper. It was hardly the most cutting-edge of questions and I felt like the girl talking about the bloody watermelon in *Dirty Dancing*. 'Could I please just pop to the Ladies as well?' was my incisive follow-up question when that was done. I'd decided that if Sarah already thought I was a complete idiot I had nothing more to lose. I might as well at least try and look good when they told me they'd made a terrible mistake and I had to leave.

I managed to follow her directions through the maze of beige corridors and found the toilets. They were a bit of a disappointment, to be honest. I imagined the City would be incredibly glamorous – little glass bowls of Japanese flowers, stacks of fluffy white hand towels, maybe scented candles and a selection of Molton Brown creams. Instead, I found dull-grey tiles, an industrial-sized soap dispenser and a scary hands-in air dryer that sounded like a Boeing 747 taking off. Fortunately, at this point all I really needed was a mirror. I took a deep breath and surveyed the damage. Hopefully it wasn't as bad as I'd feared. And it could have been worse. My hair hadn't gone frizzy and my make-up had survived the flood. Better still the ink didn't seem to have run off from the newspaper onto my face after all. I took some deep breaths to try and calm myself down. Just start the day again, Suzana. Go back in there and be yourself.

One final look in the mirror gave me the confidence to head back to the office. My suit looked good – and that meant the world to me. It was Armani. I'd sold my Volvo to pay for it the week after I'd been accepted on to this internship. I'd been convinced that everyone else in London would look a million dollars. So even though I was working almost for free, I was determined to compete. As I patted the jacket down, I tried to forget the fact that everyone else I'd seen in the building so far looked, well, very high street.

'All sorted now?' Sarah smiled as I walked back into her room. She seemed to have filled in most of the forms for me and passed them over for a signature. Please don't be waterlogged. Please work, I begged, as I got a pen out of my bag. It worked perfectly. I'd pulled myself back from the brink. I nodded frequently and tried to look fascinated as Sarah went into extraordinary detail about where to go during the fire drill and how to get into the building on a bank holiday. Hopefully she no longer thought they'd made a terrible mistake by picking me for this job. All I needed now was to find out exactly what it was.

To this day, I'm still not exactly sure what drew me to the City. Maybe a psychologist could tell me. In the spring of 2004, when I applied for my internship, I just knew that I wanted to prove a point. I was about to get a music degree from one of America's 'new Ivies' on the East Coast, Colgate University, and for some reason it felt as if everyone kept focusing on what I couldn't do. Upon graduation, career advisers seemed to segregate jobs between the sexes. Boys went for the lucrative, tough jobs. Girls should go for something nicer, more vocational and easier to quit the moment they decided to become a mum – think teacher, therapist or music historian. At one point I even read an article online that warned women against working in orchestras because the job was too physically demanding. If you work in an orchestra you'll have to work evenings, the piece pointed out. That means you'll have no social life – and by implication, no husband. Had that been written in Jane Austen's day? Amazingly not – it was brand-new advice. I clicked away and carried on with my job search.

One of my best friends at university was a tall, sexy field hockey player called Michael. He came from an incredibly wealthy family, his dad ran a bank and the career adviser had encouraged him to take his economics degree to become a 'big shot in finance'. We'd all seen *Wall Street* and *Rogue Trader* so we had a bit of an idea of what that 'big shot' might be. I'd also just read *Liar's Poker* and *The Bonfire of the Vanities,* so I should probably have spotted a few potential obstacles. In truth, though, all I got from the films and books was motivation. It all seemed fabulously exciting. There were whole worlds to conquer in the City. Too weak to play a musical instrument? Too needy to work in the evenings? I decided to prove I was strong enough to conquer the world of finance.

'I'd like to apply for the same internship that Michael is going for,' I told the career adviser when my appointment came along. It was a well-advertised, one-year internship programme at an investment bank in London. I spent my whole life dreaming of living in London. I lapped up books and films set there. I watched more British television than anyone I knew, and my music collection had already survived the 'English Invasion', with playlists full of Depeche Mode, Sting and the Beatles. That internship had my name on it. I got the application form, and worked on my 'statement of purpose' for about a week. I had a half-hour interview, kept my fingers crossed, and received the call saying I'd won the post. Michael took it pretty well, but then again, he could always go work for his father's Wall Street firm – an option I didn't have. Meanwhile, I was beside myself with excitement. I was ecstatic at the thought of going to work in London. But a tiny bit of me was even more pleased that I'd beaten one of the boys to win the chance. If only I'd known how rocky this particular route was going to be.

Fast forward to August 2004, and Sarah had moved on to explain a little more about the company. We were part of a giant, multinational investment bank, with brokers and traders working in every corner of the world. The company had a dozen buildings in London alone. Its best performers earned million-pound bonuses, and part of my job would be to process the details after those superstars completed their trades. After the low point about emergency meeting points and fire marshalls, this was starting to get spicy again. I was amazed they would let a lowly intern get so close to the action. But maybe that's the City for you. Once you're in, you're on the fast track. Clearly, in the world of finance, there is no such thing as a slow lane.

Sarah finished her spiel and took me back towards the lifts. I was on my way to security to get a photo taken for my pass card. That was where reality started to bite. I hadn't expected a Hollywood-style Winnebago and a full hair and make-up department. But if the company really did employ all these hot-shot masters of the universe, surely there would be more than a glorified Photo-me booth staffed by a guard even older than my big-nosed friend on reception? I stood in front of the white noticeboard and tried not to blink when the flash went off. I blinked.

I headed back up to the HR department with my macabre pass in my pocket. Fiona was there to meet me. 'I'll show you the staff restaurant,' she said brightly as we headed back down to the ground floor. It was certainly impressive, and Fiona proved to be a very enthusiastic guide. She became extraordinarily animated the moment we walked into the serving area. 'The food's pretty good, you load up a card with credit and everything's heavily subsidised,' she began. 'It's open for breakfast from six, there are two or three different main meals every lunchtime and it's open till nine at night as well. You can eat here or take food up to your desk. The knives and forks are over there. The trays go over there . . .'

I was nodding and smiling, trying desperately hard to appear as if I was taking it all in. Was it normal for new recruits to need help finding the cutlery? Weren't there more important things to be telling me about? If I got this much instruction about where to put my tray, then how hard would it be to log on to the intranet?

Fiona grabbed us coffees so I could see how the card system worked. She had a chat with the lady on the till, then we sat beside a fake plant to talk about all the other sandwich bars and cafés outside the building. Our conversation moved on to where we both lived. I said I was sharing a flat with some strangers over in South Kensington. She used the Northern Line to come in every day from Golders Green. Every now and then, she broke off to chat to people who walked past our table. The whole office seemed to be full of very charming, very ordinary people with all the time in the world. It's nice, I was thinking, but where's the action? Where are the slick young guys in the sharp suits? And why do I feel so overdressed?

I snapped out of my daydream as Fiona waved goodbye to one of her friends, and said it was time for me to meet my new colleagues. My whole body tensed up. Don't be nervous, I told myself. And all of a sudden, I wasn't. I was ready for the adventure to really begin.

I wanted to walk into that big City cauldron and meet the financial masters of the universe. After a whole morning feeling off-balance and out of place, I decided that I would finally feel at home.

The lift doors opened on the seventh floor, and we headed to the left. Fiona stepped aside so I could use my security pass to open the double doors that led on to a vast open-plan office with a shimmering view of the Thames. In my head I was ready to see some Gordon Gekko figure screaming at some poor subordinate who had lost him ten million pounds in a careless phone call. Instead, there was a deafening silence.

It was like walking into an ancient cathedral when you're on holiday. I think Fiona actually turned to me and put her finger on her lips in a 'shhhh' motion as we walked around the edge of the first big group of desks. Had someone just died? I was thinking. Had there been some awful tragedy in the bank and is everyone in shock? There must have been close to a hundred people in the office and I couldn't understand why no one was speaking. We crept – almost literally, crept – across the floor to a set of desks that appeared to be surrounded by a wall of photocopiers. A Chinese girl about my age was sitting right across from them. I pulled my Armani jacket a little closer. It was like I'd misread the invitation to a party and come in fancy dress. I had a horrible feeling I might have misjudged absolutely everything.

17

'I'm Marina. I've been doing the internship for the past year,' she said, a strange look of triumph in her face.

'Marina has been a big hit,' Fiona said proudly. 'She's not made a single mistake all year. She's had brilliant reviews and she's getting a great reference.'

'Are you staying with the company?' I asked. Again, there was that odd look in the girl's deep, dark eyes.

'I'm going back to school to get my MBA,' she said enigmatically.

I stood back a little and gazed out across the office as Fiona found me a chair. This wasn't anything like the fast-paced banks in the movies. Nobody was standing up and shouting. No one was conducting high-pressure discussions over the phone, let alone to each other. I couldn't understand how so many people could be making so little noise. Apart from the tapping of keyboards, it was like being in a very strict school assembly. Fiona had shown me where the Ladies was as we got out of the lift. I had an awful feeling I'd have to put my hand up and ask if I wanted to use it.

'Marina will be with you for the next two days to show you the ropes and arrange the handover,' Fiona said when she had wheeled me over a chair. That was when I had a moment of panic. I was convinced that two days couldn't possibly be enough to learn a job I'd be doing for an entire year. I'd already forgotten where the knives and forks were kept in the staff restaurant. I wasn't sure I could cope with anything else. 'I'll leave you two to it. You know where I am if you need me,'

Fiona said. I watched her walk back across the cathedral to the security doors. No! I don't know where you are if I need you! I felt like shouting. But in the click of a gleaming glass door, Fiona was gone. It was time to focus on the job.

As it turned out, Marina really could cover it all in two hours. She might well have been able to do it in twenty minutes. This set of numbers pop up on the screen here. These ones go there. These other ones need to be added up here. This final figure, here, will be the same as that final figure there. That was pretty much it.

'What if the figures aren't the same?' I asked after my first demonstration.

Marina looked blankly at me. 'What do you mean?'

'What if the figures aren't the same? What happens then?'

There was an awful silence. For some reason I could sense real confusion in her mind. 'They're always the same,' she said flatly. She gave me another odd look and shrugged.

'What else do I do, after that?' I asked, trying to lighten the mood.

'More figures come in,' Marina said. 'They come in all the time.'

'Do I need to speak to anyone about them? Maybe to check anything?'

'I never have.' We sat in silence for a while, which felt mortifyingly odd to me, but seemed to suit everyone else in the office just fine. There wasn't anyone sitting

19

in the desk directly opposite Marina, but the ones to her right were both occupied. One of the guys was an average-looking thirty-something bloke in a dark-blue, open-necked shirt.

He gave a quick smile when he stopped tapping in numbers for a moment and accidentally caught my eye. But that was it. A month ago, when I'd had this placement confirmed, my mother had sat me down at home for a thoroughly awkward chat about the evils of drugs in the big city. Yet I now got the distinct sensation that the only drug anyone took around here was Valium. I wondered idly how Michael would have coped if he'd got the placement instead of me. He was one of the loudest, most dynamic and aggressive guys I'd ever met. He wouldn't have lasted ten minutes.

At exactly 1 p.m., Marina suggested we go to lunch together. I was thrilled. I wanted to pick her brains in private, while impressing her with my uncanny ability to find cutlery and put my tray in the right place after my meal. 'Is it always so quiet up there?' I began, once we'd bought our food and found somewhere to sit.

She gave me a hint of a smile. 'It's not the most exciting job in the world,' she said hesitantly. 'It's not the worst, probably. But it never gets really wild.'

'So it really is just inputting numbers all day?'

'Yes it is. Someone has to do it. I guess, for them, it makes sense to give it to someone on an internship rather than someone on a big salary. This is a good place to have on your CV. But it's a stepping stone. It's helped me get accepted on to one of the top MBA courses. You'll be able to use it for something as well. The year does go fast, in the end.'

I didn't really like the sound of all that, to be honest. But Marina was talking about the holiday she was planning before going back to business school. She and her boyfriend were going to cycle through Thailand, Vietnam and Cambodia. I drifted away on her dreams and by the time we headed back upstairs, I realised I'd forgotten to ask about any of her colleagues. A crowded lift didn't seem the right place to gossip, so I kept quiet. On the seventh floor I edged ahead again so I could use my pass to open the security door. For some reason, that click felt good. Marina might be right and this wasn't going to be the most exciting job in the world. But at least I was in.

Ahead of us there was something else that swept away my sense of impending doom. I'd been too busy following Fiona to notice our view before. But it was spectacular. We were lower than the HR department, but we pointed in a slightly different direction. Somehow that meant we could see further. Between two buildings there was a corner of the Thames and a full-on panorama of Tower Bridge and the South Bank. All my fears evaporated as I took a long look, burning the majestic image into my heart. A tourist boat was edging in towards one of the piers while a fast clipper service was motoring away from it and heading towards Canary Wharf. I've had a bad start, I thought to myself. The rainstorm was a nightmare. The actual office is all a bit quieter than I'd expected. But I'm here, slap bang in the middle of the City of London. Men have been making their fortunes here for hundreds of years. Now it's my turn. It's all going to be fine.

Marina ran through the basics of my job again in the afternoon. It was a repeat of everything she had said in the morning. 'Do you fancy a try?' she asked. She pushed her chair away from the screen and I wheeled mine in close. I took the mouse in my right hand. At the back of my mind, I wondered if this might be some kind of test. Was it all a lot more complicated than Marina had made out? When I try it, will it be infinitely trickier and will I have to prove hidden depths of mathematical skill? It wasn't, and I didn't. Marina was right. One set of numbers went here, another set went there. The final figure at the bottom of the screen was exactly the same as the final figure at the top. 'I think you've got it,' Marina said after about ten minutes. 'Let's try it again.'

Marina and I had a quick coffee together just before she left at the end of the second handover day. I asked if she fancied a drink after work but she said she couldn't make it. It was as if she couldn't get out of the office fast enough. Perhaps that should have been a warning sign. I remember logging off what would soon be my computer at the end of that day and that I seemed to pass hundreds of packed City bars as I headed to the Tube. I'd have liked to see what they were like. I squeezed on to a Central Line train and headed west. I was sharing a tiny flat with three other girls, all French. They were old friends and worked in a science lab at Imperial College in South Kensington. Even if I'd understood their language, I don't think I'd really have known what they were talking about half the time.

I arrived ridiculously early for my third day at the bank – the first where I'd be completely on my own. My official hours were nine till six, but I got on the tube at seven-thirty for my forty-five minute trip east. I'd bought another copy of the *FT* for the journey because I thought it might look impressive. I bought a coffee in Starbucks on King William Street to wake me up after reading its editorials. Just before eight-thirty, I swiped my security pass over the sensor and headed to the lifts. The nice security guard with the nose gave me a cheery wave as I walked past.

I smiled broadly all the way up in the lift, and then I stopped. My entire floor was vacant. I walked to my desk. Was it a public holiday I was unaware of? Would everyone suddenly jump up from under their desks, shout 'surprise!' and set off streamers? I had a feeling the latter was pretty unlikely so I sat down and waited. I crunched my *FT* up a bit so it looked as if I'd read it, then put it on top of my empty in-tray. I still believed that image was important in the City. And it had cost nearly a pound, after all.

So where *was* everyone? I got my answer at exactly ten to nine. The glass doors opened and it was as if the entire payroll arrived at once. I later found out that

23

almost everyone in the office got the same trains in to London Bridge every morning, and that I was pretty much the only person who didn't live in the suburbs. Maybe they all sat with each other and laughed and joked on the trains. Maybe that was why they were so silent at work. The office had gone from empty to full within the span of fifteen minutes. But if you closed your eyes you would barely have known it. I input my numbers and checked the totals in silence for the rest of the day. I smiled at people but didn't have a single proper conversation beyond salutations and talk about the weather. Until that point, I'd thought that the idea of hearing a pin drop was just an expression. Then, at the end of my first week, I tossed the safety pin from my dry-cleaning into a bin. The nervous guy with the open-necked shirt sitting to my right looked up as if a gun had gone off. It was the first time he'd ever really moved. It appeared to be the most exciting thing that had happened to him in ages.

Lost in my sea of silence every day, I got to work. I tapped in my numbers, added up the columns and, yes, I checked that the two totals matched. Then I did it again. And again. The numbers came in on email attachments or – such a thrill – in paper files that someone actually came to my desk to drop off. 'Thank you!' I said brightly to my first messenger boy. Everyone around me looked up. The lad turned on his heel, startled.

After that I just nodded. Even a smile seemed too risky and over-familiar. Once I'd input the numbers into the right boxes I pressed 'send' and they disappeared to God knows where. I had no idea if anyone actually needed them or looked at them. Some days I wondered if it was all a total fraud. It could well be that this was a fake job set up to keep each year's bright-eyed intern quiet and fulfil some government quota. Perhaps I was only there to get someone a tax break. Then I started to become obsessed by the question I'd asked on my first day. What if the figures aren't the same? At the start of my second week of inputting I'd built this up to such an enormous degree in my head I really don't think I could have coped if they'd shown up differently. Would one of the columns go red? Might a bell go off? For some bizarre reason I had an idea that it might be like an aeroplane in turbulence. If I got one figure wrong, then masks and emergency air supplies would fall from our ceiling and Fiona from HR would rush into the office yelling, 'Brace! Brace!' as the company plunged in to despair. If only things had been so exciting.

By the end of my second week, I had made a terrible discovery. I could do my job and spend my entire day without saying a single word to another soul. I had a phone on my desk, but it may as well have been an ornament. No one ever rang in, and I never had any reason to ring out. The desk directly opposite me was empty. I had the photocopiers to my left and the two guys to my right were too busy feverishly tapping at their keyboards to come up for air. Had they even noticed that Marina had left and I'd taken over? I'd read somewhere about an office worker in Japan who had died at his desk. No one had noticed for four days. 'He was always very quiet,' his colleagues had said when they were questioned about it. If I die, how long before someone calls my parents? I wondered. I had a horrible feeling that four days might be an under-estimate.

One thing did work in my favour though: my position right next to all the photocopiers. At first, it was all a bit of a disaster. They belched out hot air and the constant grinding noise drove me mad. My desk also put me in the front line for questions. Low toner, paper jam, having trouble resizing your documents? Clearly the right course of action was to ask the girl sitting next to it. How convenient. For the first few days, I was probably quite stroppy about all that. No, I don't know what toner is, let alone where it goes. No, I have no idea if A5 is bigger or smaller than A4. And, most of all, I don't want to get ink on my lovely new suit. Don't you know what I sacrificed so I could afford this?

I changed my tune after about a week. I realised that being asked about paper jams was better than not being talked to at all. I stopped finding it demeaning to be treated like a glorified secretary, even though I had a degree from a top university. I started to be thrilled just to be treated like someone with a pulse. So after spending a week hoping that the paper wouldn't jam, I began to positively relish it. Our vast open-plan office had one youngish guy who vaguely fitted the City Boy template of my dreams. He had great hair, a decent tan and he looked rich. He even wore a proper suit with sharp pinstripes and a shirt that looked as if it cost more than twenty pounds. The first time he headed towards the copiers I was desperate to delay him. If I'd know where or what it was, I'd have burst the toner container with the heel of my shoe so I'd get the chance to talk to him. As it was, his copies thundered out of the machine without a hitch. He was gone, back to the furthest corner of our floor, a faint smell of Hugo Boss the only sign that he'd ever been there at all.

'So, how's it going?' I was in a pub a few streets behind the Tate Modern. Four other American graduates were doing similar internships in the City of London. We were meeting for the first time since our new office lives had begun. All five of us seemed to be in shock.

'It's OK,' said Robert, a remarkably intense guy straight out of Wharton Business School, who had a very distant look in his eye that night. 'It's not exactly cutting-edge stuff, but it's got potential. You have to start somewhere, right?'

'Are you doing anything, well, useful?' asked Danielle, one of the other business grads who had landed a job in a Canary Wharf investment bank.

'Define useful,' I asked.

'Well, anything that feels as if there's a point to it.

27

Anything that couldn't be done just as easily by a five-year-old or a monkey.'

'Then no.' I had to say. I'd planned to lie to everyone all night and talk up my job as if it were the most exciting thing on earth. But my spirit was already broken. When the time came, I couldn't find the energy to fake it. 'I just punch numbers into boxes on a computer screen. I add up two columns of figures. I press save and send. That's all I do. Then I do it again.'

'So what are the people like? My place is incredibly quiet. Does anyone talk to you?' Robert, by the sound of it, was in some parallel universe, mirror-image office to mine. We spent about an hour comparing horror stories of being ignored, overlooked and crushed by boredom. 'I thought working in the City was supposed to be exciting. It was in *Rogue Trader* and *Wall Street*,' I said as we headed out separate ways at the end of the night. I'd signed up to a full year at my bank but I wasn't sure I'd last till the end of the month.

# Chapter 2

THREE WEEKS INTO THE job, a Welshman saved my life. Up until now, he had been to Australia on an extended holiday. He exploded back into the office like, well, a real-life, larger-than-life City Boy. His name was Jason, he was about thirty years old, six–four, was easily better-looking than anyone else in the office apart from Hugo Boss boy, and he sat in the empty desk opposite me. Better still – he talked to me!

'So you're the new Marina,' were his first words. 'I bet you've been having a barrel of laughs here so far. Been out partying with the crew yet?' He gestured towards my two feverishly busy colleagues on the next-door desk. 'I didn't think so,' he said, without waiting for me to think of a nice way to reply.

'So, do you fancy going out for a quick drink?' he asked. I'd said 'yes' before he'd finished the question. A drink! A social drink! With someone who seemed to be alive! I reached for my jacket and stood up. 'Steady, girl! It's nine o'clock on a Monday morning. You're a goer, aren't you? I meant a drink tonight, after work.'

I went so red I thought I might lose consciousness. I slumped back in my chair and tried to laugh. 'Just testing,' was all I could think of to say. For the rest of the day whenever I looked over at Jason, he was smirking, but I didn't actually care. I was beside myself with excitement at the thought of finally making it into one of the City bars. Thank God for Jason, I kept telling myself. And thank God for my Armani. I'm finally going to have a laugh and fit in somewhere.

At 6 p.m on the nose, we went to a boat moored on the Thames just upstream from our office. It was a warm August evening and we bagged the corner of a big table up on the deck and watched the sun set over the luminescent river. The boat was packed with cool-looking people all of whom seemed to be going somewhere in their careers and their lives. They seemed busy, satisfied – everyone looked focused and successful. Jason ordered us two big glasses of white wine and we chinked them as my official welcome to the office.

'So, how do you like Jurassic Park?' he asked as he pulled off his jacket.

'I'm sorry?'

'Our lovely colleagues. The fossils. Made any life-long friends yet?'

I wasn't sure what to say. I had this feeling he might be testing me, so I kept things light. I didn't want to be mean about anyone, then discover he'd been the best man at their wedding. He smiled. He had great teeth.

'Look, you can cut the bullshit. I've never worked with as many boring dullards in my entire life. And I've been an accountant for nearly a decade. You've been there, what, three weeks? Then you'll want to let off steam. Tell me what you really think.'

'It's a little bit quiet,' I offered.

'It's as quiet as the bloody grave.'

'Well, it's got better since you arrived today.'

He smiled. 'Well, that's how it's going to stay. I probably drive everyone mad in that place, but they drive me mad as well so it evens out. It can be you and me against the lot. Marina was nice, but she wasn't really up to making waves. I need to sit opposite someone who's got a bit of a spark.'

I was wildly flattered he felt that person could be me. We had a great night on the boat. I was staggering a bit after four glasses of wine and nothing to eat when we headed back over the gangplank and towards our separate Tube stations. Jason had shown me pictures of his girlfriend so I knew this hadn't been a pseudo-date and didn't make some ghastly gaffe by acting as if it was. Instead, it was the start of an office friendship. I knew next to nothing about office life at that point. But I already had a feeling that this would make it a million times better than it had been so far.

The next day, I timed my arrival for exactly ten to nine, along with the rest of the commuting herd. It was one small way I'd managed to fit in. Jason arrived right alongside me. He was talking before he'd slung his jacket on the back of his chair. He didn't let up all day or indeed any day. He talked constantly. It was like listening to the radio. Even the nervous, feverishly typing men around us had to join in sometimes. I loved every nonsensical minute of it. Jason joked about girls, sport, television programmes, films, anything that floated into his head. Better still – he started to flirt with me. We both seemed to know it was never serious. The girl-friend in the holiday photos sort of put paid to that. But it was a wonderful distraction from the Excel spread-sheets. I adored all the lecherous glances he threw in my direction. Sometimes I threw a few back. I laughed at all his suggestive comments and silly jokes. After about a month, I'd forgotten how awful the first three weeks of my internship had been. I was still desper-ately lonely at home with my three French flatmates though, so I actually looked forward to getting back to my desk every day.

Jason's role was pretty similar to mine, frighteningly so, bearing in mind the fact that he got paid and had been doing it for so much longer than me. He tapped in different numbers for a different department and, to be fair, he did work hard between all the clowning around. He also taught me how to handle our boss, a nightmare of a man called Anthony who seemed desperate to find fault with everything everyone did. He was very posh, very old school, and I'd have put money on him being in his early fifties. He was, in fact, thirty-seven. I'd had one very unwelcoming welcome meeting with him in my first week. He had called me into his office, barely looked away from his screen and seemed deeply annoyed that I'd not made any mistakes so far. 'You're going to have to watch it,' he warned, clearly displeased with me. 'I'll expect things to stay this way. This job is no easy ride. Please remember that.' Then I was dismissed and sent back out into the silence. Welcome aboard. Not.

Anthony could be just as negative when he paced the office floor and spoke to people at their desks. I cringed sometimes at the things he said to the feverishly typing guys to my right. No wonder the poor souls were so jumpy. But I was fascinated by the way Jason responded to Anthony. He played the fool even more when the boss was around. He would lean so far back in his chair that he was almost horizontal. He pretended to be spaced-out when he was asked a direct question. And he got away with it. That was my first real lesson of the City: if you're good at your job, you can act as badly as you want and no one will care. As long as the numbers come out right, then you can get away with anything. I stored that little fact away in my mind in case I needed it later.

As the weeks passed, Jason's comedy act got even more sophisticated. He went into overdrive when our month-end figures coincided with some important quarterly Profit and Loss (or P&L) reports. That meant even more numbers than normal had to be tapped into even more flashing boxes on our screens. Jason would work in silence for two or three hours at a stretch – something I'd never seen him do before. Then he'd pretend to be having a nervous breakdown. He'd fake some heavy breathing. He'd roll his head and eyes around and let his tongue flop out of the corner of his mouth like a human Labrador. Sometimes he'd even fall straight out of his chair and begin flapping like a fish on the floor. To my surprise, others joined in. Not with the flapping on the floor, or the rolling of the eyes. But with a few smiles and laughs. Everyone was working overtime and putting in ten or twelve-hour days. But despite the office adversity, we finally began to bond.

It was late November when I realised that Jason had bewitched me. He had made the world's dullest job seem bearable. When I had begun the placement, I'd not expected to last a month. Now I had lasted nearly four. Some of the time, it had even been a laugh.

We went out drinking a couple of nights a week and one time I berated him for what he'd done. 'You've institutionalised me,' I said accusingly. 'You've brainwashed me and made me forget who I am. You've taken a country girl with an Armani suit and turned her into a robot. I hate you.'

He just smiled. 'It's Stockholm Syndrome, when kidnap victims fall in love with their kidnappers. We all knew we could break you down in the end. We did it to poor, dear Marina. We'll have you living in the suburbs before you know it. You'll be elbowing your way between the thousands of London Bridge worker drones every morning at eight-thirty.'

We'd talk about all the ways my life could shrink and become ever more ordinary. But as December came and I planned a trip back to my parents in America, I started to lose my sense of humour. Maybe I *had* been institutionalised. I looked up Stockholm Syndrome on the internet and the description did seem uncannily accurate. I wanted to run banks like a modern-day Rothschild. Would I end up robbing them like Patty Hearst?

My more immediate worry was what I'd say to my parents when they asked me how the job was going. Their idea of investment banking was the same as mine had been – a manic world of thrusting, shouting, successful traders. They imagined a thrilling, fast-moving casino full of larger than life *Wall Street*-style personalities where only the strongest survive. Sure, they knew I was only on a sort of glorified internship, but they still assumed I was right there in the middle of it, testing and proving myself every day and coming home each night exhausted, stressed-out, but infinitely stronger. How could I explain the mind-numbing reality?

The only good news I had to offer them was that by December I wasn't just inputting figures. Sometimes I got to plot them in a graph as well. Looking back, I can't believe how big a thrill that little development had been. Or that it would soon get even better. 'Can you do pivot tables?' one of my colleagues asked one morning.

'I can try,' I said. It turned out that they were easy – and gave me a ridiculously elevated sense of achievement. From then on, I helped out with several other computer packages, put together some even bigger spreadsheets and generally tried to make myself as useful as possible. I also tried to get a sense of what it was all for. These numbers aren't just numbers, I reminded myself as I punched them in each day. They're the results of trades that have been going on in another part of this company. They're the proof that the real City does exist and that someone, somewhere, is doing something exciting.

That thought became my lifeline. I became obsessed by the belief that through another set of lift doors I'd find the wild and passionate side of the City. I just needed to know which button to press when I got in the lift.

I decided to ask for more information in my half-year review. Anthony's secretary called me into one of the meeting rooms just after eleven one morning. He had very cruelly positioned himself with his back to the windows. I was left bleached-out and exposed by the light. Position is power, I thought to myself. Next time I'm in a meeting I'm getting to the room first and I'm sitting right where you are.

Anthony began with a little recap of my role. His skin, flattered by the softer light, looked surprisingly soft. I still couldn't believe he was only thirty-seven though. I wondered if he was married. Apart from Jason, all the men seemed to be. Even the least attractive of them appeared to have found someone to drag to the altar. Somewhere, there must be a pool of women with very low standards, I realised. I wondered what the wives looked like; no one had family photos on their desks. Though there was a guy near the door who had a framed picture of a car on his. He too was married, amazingly.

'As you know, compliance is a serious job and it needs serious people.' I snapped back to the here and now. Anthony had been talking for ages. Was the meeting nearly over? 'If you're to be offered a position here in the future, you will need to prove you are meticulous, detail-oriented and deliberate.' He was looking at my file. 'You've done very well, so far, but you can't be complacent. Compliance has no place for complacency.' He smiled at that little witticism. I smiled back. The things you do to keep the boss happy. 'So, if there's nothing you want to ask?' he said, pushing my papers back into their file.

'There is something,' I said. I'd rehearsed the next bit for ages, but the words still came out as both rushed and stilted. 'Would it be possible for me to see more of the company and the work that it does? I'd like to meet some of the people who carry out the trades that I work on. I think it would give me a better picture of what we all do here. I'd happily make up any hours in the evenings or at the weekend if I could spend a day or so in a few other departments once in a while.'

Anthony looked right at me. I realised he'd never done that before. He normally looked at his screen, his paperwork or at some point just past my right shoulder. To be honest, I was so nervous that day that I can't quite remember what he said. I had this horrible feeling

37

that using the words 'other departments' was banned by some obscure compliance by-law. But while I never did get to meet any of the front office traders, or find out exactly what the numbers on my computer screen represented, Anthony did start to involve me in more of our team's work.

Just after Christmas he asked me to sit in on a meeting with some of our IT staff. There were five of us in his office and I was left to squeeze onto the very end of his sofa. I can't actually remember what we talked about. I was too busy trying to stay upright. Later on, I started to go to some of the weekly meetings Anthony called with each of his section managers. We ran through endless pages of figures, everyone always agreed with everything everyone else said, and we left the room having achieved precisely nothing. If this is management then count me in, I thought. As long as you get your own chair, it's a piece of cake.


By February, I was an old hand at the meetings culture. I had also started to get more than a little bit bored. I had gradually perfected the art of arriving first, choosing the best seat, and always saying something very early on so I didn't look like the idiot in the corner who was too scared to speak. I also spotted that people were impressed if you took notes, though mine weren't strictly orthodox. First, I'd make sure that no one could actually see my notepad. Then, whenever anyone said anything that sounded vaguely important, I'd write a bit more of my latest shopping list or jot down a few more things I wanted to do at the weekend. I got quite good at doodling as well.

'Another love-in with the management?' Jason would say as I left my desk, pad in hand, for each meeting.

'Yes, and your bad behaviour is the first item on the agenda,' I'd tell him.

I tried to wind him up about some of my away days as well. In the spring, the people who had organised my work placement set up a series of events at Henley Business School, City University, and at colleges in Oxford and Cambridge. Most of the meetings were as dull as ditchwater. But at least they got me away from my desk. 'I'm going in the company jet,' I'd tell Jason. 'One of the chauffeurs is coming to pick me up at midday' I'd say. 'They're putting me up in a five-star hotel in the country so I won't be back till Monday.'

In these stupid jokes about the high life, a silly little dream was born. I incorporated the exaggerations with Jason into a new, secret life. I decided to change who I was the moment I got away from my desk. I started to become someone else in the lift on the way down to the atrium. I was a totally different person by the time I got out on to King William Street and headed towards the Tube. Outside the office, I was City Girl. These people don't know that all I do all day is crunch meaningless numbers. They don't know that I'm not even getting paid. They can only see my Armani suit. They think I'm a success. I walked taller, even though I'm only five–four. I clicked my heels a little louder. I tried to look fierce, confident, and supremely busy. And I loved it.

'I think I want to be a trader.' The words came out when Jason and I were in one of our usual haunts on Lombard Street. It was a Thursday night in March. We'd spent half an hour talking rubbish when I made my announcement. Jason just looked at me. Then he smiled. Then he rolled his eyes and shrugged.

For the first time since I'd met him, I wanted to hit him. It was as if he was mocking me. That was against our rules. We could laugh about everyone else in the office but not each other. Not about something as serious as this.

'I mean it. I want to be a trader,' I said, desperately hoping stupid tears didn't form in my eyes. That was when Jason did something lovely. He reached across the table and took my hand in his. It wasn't sexual, or flirtatious, or silly. It was kind and compassionate and I've never forgotten it. 'Do you know anything about trading?' he asked, once he'd calmed me down and my hand was back in my lap. I smiled weakly. Then I started to talk. All my unfocused thoughts and dreams poured out of me. I kept talking for nearly an hour. Poor Jason couldn't have known what hit him.

'I know that they're in the thick of things. They make

the money, they're the reason people like us have to do what we do. Look, I'm twenty-three, this is my first job, and it only lasts till the end of the summer. I need to plan my next move soon and I don't see why I shouldn't aim for the top. I love working with you, but I can't end up in another office like this one. I need to get out and I want to do a proper job. One where I get respect and make money and achieve something real. I've researched everything and trading is my answer. It's what I want to do.'

We ordered another bottle of wine and I explained a little more about my dreams of becoming a proper City Girl. 'Do you know any traders? Has your course given you any ideas about how you could get into that part of the business?' Jason asked at the end of our night.

The answers were 'no' and 'no'.

'Well, let's see what we can do tomorrow morning,' Jason said before heading off to London Bridge station. 'We'll start "project trader" at 9 a.m. sharp.' What a total star he was.

# Chapter 3

JASON KICKED OFF 'PROJECT trader' by letting me in on a secret. It seemed that our computer passwords gave us access to a full staff directory for the company. I plundered it. I mined it for anyone who had any remote connection to anywhere I'd ever lived or studied, to anything I'd ever done. If I thought I had a link to anyone, I wrote all their details down. Then, when 'project trader' moved into its next phase, I took my mobile out into the street, took a deep breath and rang them up.

Some of them were super-important people. Looking back, I can't believe I had the nerve to call them. For a while, I thought I was going to be thwarted. 'And it's in connection with what, exactly?' their harsh-voiced secretaries would ask me, time and again. 'Just so I am clear on this, does he know you or not?'

'I just want ten minutes of his time,' I'd beg. 'I can come along whenever is convenient to him. I just want to talk about my opportunities within the company.' In the end, just two gate-keeper secretaries gave me access to their bosses. Out of maybe a dozen different calls, I had two meetings set up.

I knew I had to make the most of them. I'd been reading up on traders and the way they fitted into the city every night for the past couple of weeks. When my number-crunching allowed I'd read about them online at the office as well. The more I learned the more intrigued I became. These guys – and they all seemed to be guys – were at the top of the tree. They were the ones everyone in the company had to look up to. They had the most responsibility and the biggest lives. The literature all focused on the quick decisions they had to make and all the opportunities and investment trends they had to spot. I genuinely thought I could do the same. It wasn't just about making money for myself. It wasn't just defying everyone's expectations of what a girl with a music degree could do. It was more about being right at the heart of things. And now I had a couple of meetings set up I could move that little bit closer.

How long can one good suit last? I was wearing mine sparingly now. I was earning some extra cash in the evenings by babysitting and giving piano lessons in Clerkenwell. But a year of barely paid internship experience was draining my savings faster than I'd expected. I'd not bought any new clothes all year. Not even in Next. But I splashed out before I headed to the bank's St Paul's office for my first meeting with a fund manager I'd called because he came from the same town as my mother back in the American Midwest. She didn't know him, of course, but she told me he was bound to want to see me. Thanks, Mum, for being right. I didn't want to try and somehow trade on my looks but I did want to look good so I spent forty-five pounds on a new hairdresser. It's always a gamble to try someone new, especially before a big occasion, but I was ready to take risks. I also had my nails done and doubled the amount of make-up I usually wore. If anyone in the office had ever really looked at me, they'd surely have spotted that something was up. No one did.

'Break a leg,' Jason told me in a good-luck email just before I headed to St Paul's. 'In these heels that's a distinct possibility.' I typed as my reply.

Maybe I was naive, but I had decided to take the direct approach when I met this first City gent. I didn't want to get bogged down with small talk. If time is money, then I might as well get straight to the point. 'I want to be a trader,' I told him bluntly as I sat down in his office. 'I'm hoping you could advise me on how to do it.'

I tried to stay calm and neither blush nor flinch as he looked me up and down. I couldn't read his face at all. Maybe that was a skill you needed on the trading floor, just like at the poker table. Ask me anything about trading, I was saying to myself. Test me on my knowledge of the company and the City. I've researched this. I know how it all works and how everything fits in. Just ask me. But he didn't. A tiny smile played on his lips and it seemed as if he wanted to do all the talking. 'Your maths has to be the best. Traders need to be able to discount cash flows in their sleep. Banks want people who see their jobs as the most lucrative sudoku puzzles in the world. Traders need to be fierce, flexible, dynamic. They need to think very, very fast. They need total self-confidence and self-belief. They need to be able to take any number of knocks, to thrive on confrontation, to dare to be different. They need boundless energy. The pace is punishing, the hours are worse. The rewards are high, but they're only shared by the small number of players who really thrive. Most people who think they want to be traders don't last the course. And you really, really think that's the life you want?'

It was obvious that he wanted to put me off. He thought he was painting a terrible picture of a trader's life. But then he didn't know the reality of how grim it was back in the dead zone of back-office life. For some reason, I'd lapped up his every word. I loved the sound of trading. I wanted the energy and that buzz. 'That is absolutely the life I want,' I said, surprising myself with how right the words sounded.

'Well then, tell me about your qualifications and your family background,' he said. I panicked. I didn't have an MBA from a fancy university. I didn't have a rich grandfather who had founded a bank a hundred years ago. I had a horrible feeling that I couldn't offer this man a single thing. I rattled something off about my degree – without going so far as to admit it was in music – and then focused on the work I was currently doing in compliance. I wanted to show that I'd been learning on the job and that nothing about the City had passed me by.

'It all sounds absolutely fascinating,' he said suddenly, cutting me off. In a moment of total clarity I felt as if I could read his mind. I could see what he thought of me – a twenty-something blonde, out of her depth and possibly out of her mind.

'I'm tougher than I look,' I blurted out, interrupting and probably scaring the hell out of him.

'I'm sure you are, and I really do wish you well,' he said, nonchalantly. But then he stood up. The fifteen minutes allotted to me were up and I was being sent on my way. I left the office in St Paul's and headed back towards London Bridge. I'd had such high hopes for that meeting. At the end of it, I handed over my CV and he promised to pass it to the right people in the HR department. I had the feeling he binned it the moment I'd left the office. By the time I'd left the building, I think he'd probably forgotten all about me. He had met me out of politeness, out of boredom or to just because his secretary had begged him to get me off her back. Now he had seen me, and knew I had no valuable City contacts or inside information to trade. Plus, of course, I was a girl. I already sensed that in the City you could hardly get lower down the food chain than that.

Jason raised his eyebrows as I got back to my desk. I shrugged across at him and pulled a hand through my ridiculously expensively done hair. I looked at my lovely newly painted nails as my hand hovered over my keyboard. It seemed a crime to use those nails to input meaningless figures. But I logged on and did it anyway. So, whose trades am I recording today? I asked myself as the afternoon dragged on. Who's out there living the dream and doing the job while I'm just adding up their numbers? I'd sometimes try to picture the traders getting angry and getting rich in some much nicer office. Most of my imaginary dealers were young, handsome and male. Few were women. None ever looked like me – blond, long hair, slim. It's funny how I got that right, even at the start.

I couldn't even afford a blow-dry when my second and last 'project trader' interview came up. I'd spotted the name of a guy who had been to my university and I'd played the 'alumni' card to get him to see me. His name was Simon and he was one of the most profitable sales traders in the bank. He asked me to meet him in the lobby of his building, right in the heart of the Broadgate complex by Liverpool Street Station. Behind the security desk there was a vast iron sculpture about four storeys high. In front of it a scattering of leather sofas were grouped around blue glass tables. I was guided to one of them, directly underneath a bank of TV screens showing news and finance channels and big clocks telling the time around the world. Everyone rushing past seemed to be young, sharp and smartly dressed. There was a buzz and a sense of purpose about the place that we never had at my London Bridge office. I was terrified. But I still felt confident about my prospects. This meeting could hardly go any worse than the last one.

Simon turned out to be the trader from central

casting. He was wearing a harsh pinstriped suit, a wildly striped shirt and tie and – I swear to God – a pair of braces. Success seemed to be seeping out of his pores. I could see it in his eyes. It was intoxicating. His manner was just as invigorating. 'No point in getting coffee. I've got less than five minutes. We're just going to talk here,' he said when he'd found me in the atrium. It was an abrupt, anti-social way to introduce himself, but I loved it. How nice not to bother with small talk. How liberating not to have to discuss the weather. I got a rush from the fact that this was business, pure and simple. This really was the world I wanted. In this world your sex or your style wouldn't matter. Only the numbers would.

'So, you think you want to trade?' he asked, as we sat on the leather sofa. I saw a tiny smile on his face, the same as the guy in St Paul's. All my good feelings suddenly disappeared. I was being patronised, yet again. I'm twenty-three, not twelve, I wanted to say. How often do I need to say that I'm tougher than I look?

'I know I want to trade and I know I'll be good at it,' I said. 'I just need help getting in.'

This time the smile on his face grew and I allowed myself to hope. My man at St Paul's had dismissed me at this point. This man seemed a tiny bit more engaged. 'Interesting,' he said, his eyes narrowing. It was as if he'd decided I might actually be worth a bet. 'Let me tell you what we do here.' He raced through a description of the emerging markets, fixed income, commodities, and proprietary trading teams. He said when, where and how they worked. He even managed to explain a little bit about what exactly they did. Then he stood up. 'Fancy seeing a trading floor?' he asked.

'I'd love to.'

We headed over to the lifts and squeezed in amidst a crush of very smart suits. Forget the high street. This was Jermyn Street, perfumed by the men's fragrance centre in Selfridges. The tiny lift felt like my spiritual home, and I was fizzing with excitement. Simon had begun the meeting saying he only had five minutes. Now he was giving me a tour of the building. That must mean I was close. When we got to the seventeenth floor, we turned right, then Simon used his pass to open the security doors. That was where all similarities ended between his office and mine. The noise was the first thing that hit me. The noise and the mess. We were suspended in the sky above London, but with so many screens hanging from the ceiling, we could have been in a cave. 'My boys are over there,' Simon said with alacrity as we headed into the pit. 'Boys' was the right word – because of their behaviour as much as their sex. None of them were doing any work. Instead they were making paper aeroplanes and throwing them at some poor sod in the corner. He was fending them off and trying to throw as many back as possible. It was juvenile and unprofessional and as I watched, I had just one thought in my mind: this office rocks!

I shook a few hands, got hit by a couple of paper aeroplanes, then got led towards the relative calm near the office windows. 'They'll maybe play silly buggers

49

for five more minutes, but then it's back to business. They're letting off steam because we've had a good morning and we're expecting an even better afternoon. Don't let the fun stuff fool you. We fight wars up here every day. The trick is to win more than we lose.'

I could sense my face was flushed as I was led back towards the elevators. 'I'm sure we've scared you off for good,' Simon said at the security doors. Surely he must have known he'd done the opposite? As I held out my hand to say goodbye, he said the one thing I'll never forget. 'It's been nice showing you around, but if you've learned nothing else today, it's that trading is no job for a girl.' I don't know where that came from but in that single sentence, the die was cast. This man had fooled me – he'd made me think he was helping me, when in fact he was just having a joke at my expense. When he rejoined his boys back upstairs they would probably all roar with laughter about me. I walked very tall as I left his building. If I'd been keen to trade before, I was desperate now. One day, I wanted to go to war with this very man on a trading floor. And I wanted to win.

# Chapter 4

I WAS IN THE final month of my internship and 'project trader' had got me precisely nowhere. I had exhausted my contacts, and I hadn't really got anywhere with the two I'd managed to pursue. The St Paul's guy had clearly forgotten all about me, and Paper-Plane man probably thought I was at home crying into my shoes.

Fiona and Sarah in my HR department didn't seem to think I could get any kind of internal transfer, but they did offer me a great reference in case I wanted to try my luck with a rival. I did. Fortunately, the City was doing OK in the early summer of 2005. Things weren't great, but we were expecting a second consecutive year of market growth. Some people were starting to say the whole Dot Com crisis could be forgotten and we'd soon be back above the all-time highs of 1999. Trading jobs still seemed off-limits to someone like me. But for one brief moment in the City's history, it seemed you didn't need connections or top business degrees to get a lowlier role. I signed up with a recruitment agency near the Bank of England and had a big interview set up within three days. I was thrilled and ready to play a long game. My plan now was to earn a decent wage and find out how the City really worked. Then I could capture the crown from the inside.

'So, you're really leaving. Just like all the others,' Jason asked, pretending to sulk when I told him about my upcoming interview over a bottle of our usual Pinot Grigio on the boat. 'I just hope your replacement is a bit nicer.' Strangely, she was – at least as far as Jason was concerned. It was my turn to do the two-day handover in August and I remember seeing Jason's eyes light up as Fiona led the new girl across the floor to our pod of desks. Her name was Kate, she had big innocent brown eyes, long dark hair and was cute as a button. Jason had just split up from his girlfriend in Kent and he was dating Kate within a month.

My interview with the head-hunter was surreal. 'It's CDO administration,' my recruiter had said when I popped into the office to get the background. I had nodded and smiled. I had a music degree, for God's sake. What the hell did 'CDO' stand for and why did it need administering? I looked it up online at home and learned a few paragraphs of information almost off by heart. In the actual interview the simple act of reciting those paragraphs made the two people across the desk think I was some kind of genius. How fabulous. It was slightly harder to persuade them that I was a meticulous, detail-oriented plodder. But those appeared to be the skills that they required so I started to talk a little slower and tried to fake it. It must have worked because they offered me the job the following day. If I wanted it I could start within the week. My first lesson was that when the City moves, it moves dangerously fast.

The office was a little further east than my old one, close to the approach to Tower Bridge rather than London Bridge. It was bigger – there must have been two hundred people on my floor. And while it wasn't quite as mad and exciting as the trading floor in Broadgate, it made up for it in other ways.

'I think almost everyone is having an affair with everyone else,' I told Jason when we caught up over a drink at the end of my first week. 'Everyone's married and they all live out in the country, but there's definitely a lot more than papers shuffling behind the filing cabinets. It's like *Brief Encounter*, with longing looks and meaningful glances and everyone else trying to pretend they don't notice.'

'So what's the actual work like? Did you find out what a CDO is and why it matters?'

Those were slightly harder questions to answer. One of the men from my interview had met me on my first day, sorted out my security passes and shown me to my desk. Then I was pretty much left to my own devices. I got next to no training – which I soon realised was because I'd genuinely convinced them in my interview that I knew what I was talking about. Basically, I was sat down in a little low-walled cubicle, signed on and expected to start work. I looked at the various packages on my computer screen, the paperwork in my in-tray and panicked.

The colleague in the cubicle nearest to me was an

older man in his late thirties or early forties. He seemed painfully shy, but helped out enormously. As soon as I'd been abandoned at my desk I turned to him. 'Help!' I said, hoping he would think it was funny. 'I'm not really sure what I'm supposed to be doing,' I confessed. He clicked a couple of files closed on his screen, then pulled his chair across towards mine. I had the impression that if I'd tried to engage him in chit-chat, he'd have run a mile. But talking about work was fine. He spent about twenty minutes showing me what my predecessor had done. I took pages of notes and thanked him profusely. 'If there's anything else, just ask,' he said as he wheeled himself back to his own desk. I realised I didn't even know his name.

CDOs – aka, collateralised debt obligations – aren't easy to explain and lots of people in the City who should understand them probably don't. They were introduced in the 1980s, and are basically packages of debt instruments that can be sliced, diced, rated, re-rated and sold on ad infinitum. They were some of the most risky investments that made people rich in the good times, but would come back and bite us all when the credit crunch hit. My job was to record the way we sliced, diced, rated, re-rated and sold them. In some ways it was just number crunching again but in others it was a lot more important. I got to speak to other people in other departments so I got a better picture of the way the whole process worked. Over time I ended up talking to investment managers, portfolio managers, brokers and all sorts of other people whose roles defied description. Bit by bit I built up my picture of how the investment world pulled together – and why sometimes it might hit a bump in the road. When the information I was given didn't always add up I knew who to call to find out why. I could predict which team might have missed something out and why. It felt good to see beyond my computer screen at last. But I was always wanting more. I wanted to see my contacts face to face rather than just talking on the phone. But that still seemed to be off limits. The City still put up huge barriers between its different staff. I had an online phone directory that gave me everyone's extensions but not their actual locations. I didn't even know if the people I spoke to were in my building or in another office altogether. In the canteen, the lobby and the lifts, I'd stare at people, trying to size them up. Had I spoken to them on the phone? Were any of them masters of the universe? Did they have yachts in Monte Carlo and red Ferraris to drive at the weekend? Tragically, my conclusion was normally 'no'. I was earning a wage at last and working in a bigger office. But it was still a long way from where I really wanted to be.

My floor was divided up into about four different teams who all looked after different types of CDOs. Most of these were less complicated, 'vanilla' forms of packaged debt and some were quite exotic. But all required the same thing of their human controllers: an awful lot of tapping on keyboards. On a bad day, when I didn't have to talk to any other teams on the phone, I would be glued to my screen for hours at a time. I'd come up for air and look around me. Everyone else had their heads down in their little factory farm cubicles as well. We were all staring at our screens, tapping away furiously and pushing piles of paper from one side of our desks to the other. We were all busy, busy, busy from dawn till dusk. But was there really a point to it all? Sometimes I felt as if it might not really matter if one of us didn't turn up one day. Or even if none of us turned up. Sometimes I went back to my old theory that the City was just an elaborate fake, a gravy train of people pretending to do important work when nothing was actually being produced. In Soviet Russia, hadn't they paid people to shovel snow from one side of the street to another and then paid others to move it right back? Put the workers in an office, replace the snow with numbers and Excel formulas, and wasn't this exactly the same?

I tried to snap out of it by going back to 'project trader'. Knowledge is power, I told myself. I needed to learn what was really going on in the City. I forced myself to speak to strangers in the staff restaurant, the coffee area, the water cooler, even in the lifts. I was that awful colleague who sits next to you on the Tube and talks about the office when all you want to do is forget about your day. I embarrassed myself almost constantly. But I did learn. After several weeks of networking, I had a proper mental map of the way the City worked. I knew this would make me a stronger candidate if I did ever get an interview for a new role. At its most basic level, I'd learned about the front office, middle office and back office functions. No surprise that my internship had been purely back office: no-man's-land. My current job was middle office: purgatory. The traders were front office: as far as I was concerned, the Holy Grail. Some big investment companies had all three different functions in the same vast building. Others split the teams across many different sites all over the City. My old firm separated their divisions as such, which was why we never had any slick, ambitious types in our midst. My company had fewer sites, so there was a bit of action in our building. Unfortunately my security card didn't work on those floors. And it seemed as if I wouldn't get anywhere, even if it did.

My shy desk neighbour, whose name turned out to be Tony, looked set to become my new Jason. We sat together at lunch most days, though first of all we struggled to find anything in common to talk about. He didn't open up about his personal life and I didn't actually have much of one to discuss. So we fell back on the office staple: our colleagues and our career prospects. Tony proved to be surprisingly observant. There was next to nothing about the office affairs he hadn't noticed. He made me laugh as he gossiped about our supervisors and bosses. But he gave me a bit of a shock when I told him I wanted to be promoted. 'It probably won't happen,' he began. 'You can't move up in a role like this. You can get promoted to supervisor or manager on our floor. But you won't get into the front office, at least not into the kind of roles you want.'

'But why not? If the company knows I'm here and they know I'm good, why wouldn't they promote me?'

'Because the people in the front office look down on us and wouldn't accept us in their team. They assume we're not as bright as them, and they take it as a given that we're not as talented, ambitious or smart. The only people they respect are those who are parachuted in from other companies. Their backgrounds don't matter. But it does matter if you were a nobody in the same firm yesterday. That's how you'll stay for ever. I like our office. It's a decent salary, good hours, an OK place to work. But it is a dead end.'

'Well, thanks for the pep talk,' I said, losing my appetite and pushing my tray away from me. I couldn't believe that such a quiet, nice guy could have such sadness inside of him. I wondered just when and how his career dreams had been shattered. But I had to admit – he was right. Our office proved that if you wanted a real promotion, the only way was out. I'd been invited to a big leaving do in my first week and found that these were almost weekly occurrences. People were always leaving. It was all part of the merry-go-round that played out in the City when times were good. Every bank or investment firm wanted to poach staff from their rivals. At my level, people jumped ship just to add a few extra thousands to their salaries. There was zero loyalty, and however many tears were shed at a leaving do, it seemed that once the night was over, we never heard from those people again. I soon realised that Jason and I, still drinking buddies though we no long worked together, were the exceptions to the rule. No one else ever seemed to stay in touch with old colleagues. It made the whole City office atmosphere a strange mix of sociability and anonymity, and if it wasn't for Tony, I think I might have cried with loneliness. It was hard to get close to people when you never knew if anyone would still be around from one month to the next. I'd already got to like at least two people who subsequently handed in their notice and disappeared who knows where. You don't work in the City if you want to make lifelong friends, I decided. You do it for two things: the money and for the buzz. It was high time I found them.

I got lucky one night in a wine bar in Leadenhall Street. I had gone with Tony and a group of our colleagues in the CDO team. It was a sizzling Tuesday night, and for once it wasn't a leaving do. Those were always on Thursdays or Fridays. The bar was packed and some serious money was being spent. 'Traders,' one of the guys said, annoyed, as if this was a bad thing. 'Fabulous,' I think I replied. But would I dare to speak to any of them? It turned out I didn't have to. I was a young, single blonde. So they approached me. It was like some David Attenborough nature film, a swarm of pinstriped predators swooping down on some innocent victim. Trust me, girls, if you're feeling ignored and marginalised at work, then head to a busy City bar on a midweek evening. You can even leave your purse behind. The guys are so desperate to impress their colleagues they'd rather die than let you buy a drink.

What else did I learn that night? That as a City Girl you'll never have the right job. If you're a secretary you'll be seen in only one way: as an easy lay. If you're in a middle office role like me, you could possibly be seen as an easy lay as well. But you'll also be dismissed or patronised as a loser, whatever you say or look like. If you've actually got a similar job to theirs, I had the impression you would be seen as a threat to the status quo, a threat that had to be neutralised. I kept quiet about my cripplingly dull CDO portfolios that night. I tried to build up a nice little mystique about myself, pitching myself just high enough to get some respect, but low enough to keep them interested. I was City Girl again and it felt great.

I wanted to go back to that bar the following week, but none of my colleagues were up for it. Jason said it was 'too City' as well. He was always happier on the river boats where traders in suits didn't totally dominate the show. I realised I'd also lost touch with the other Americans who were on the one-year City internship. One year later, and I seemed to be the only one who was still in London, let alone in the City. I wondered what they thought about me. On paper, I probably looked like a bit of a success. I'm glad they didn't know how lost I felt.

In November I had a chance to turn things around and make new friends. The company decided to send us all out to the country for a team-building day. 'Dress up warm and be prepared to get muddy!!!' the memo said. I didn't like the look of those three exclamation marks one bit. But I was thrilled at the thought of getting away from my desk. I was also keen to see what my colleagues wore outside the office. Would we look like commandos, hikers, or gap-year travellers? In the end we looked like accountants on an off-site excursion. I should have known.

I sat next to one of the secretaries on the coach to Sussex. Her name was Sasha, she was about my age, had nicely bobbed hair, and always wore really interesting ethnic jewellery in the office. I'd talked to her briefly at a few leaving parties and thought she seemed good fun. I was right. 'I looked this place up online and it costs more than £800 per person per day for the experience,' she said. 'If they're spending this much on us now, imagine how much they'll spend at the

Christmas party. This is going to be a very good year.'

'What are the Christmas parties like?'

'Lavish. Last year we took over an old warehouse by Brick Lane and we had a catwalk show with professional models, a champagne bar, amazing food and great live music. It went on till about one in the morning and they paid for everyone's taxi home, even the people who live way out in Essex. It was brilliant.'

'Do we get Christmas bonuses?' For some reason that had never occurred to me before. But this was the City. Bonuses were what it was all about, right?

'None of us get them. They only go to the traders and the front office people. They get their money in January.'

'Are any of them coming today?'

'They might be. Apparently someone from HR said we'd be competing against other departments. The big traders might not be able to leave during market hours. But maybe some of the juniors will be coming down. We should keep our eyes open. I could do with a rich new boyfriend.'

Unfortunately, we didn't get much chance to look around. The moment we arrived, we were whisked off to a changing room and handed a pair of gloves and protective helmets. Both items worried me slightly. Then we were divided up into four teams and sent to little huts in different corners of a vast field for 'basic training'. We did some map-reading and had a quick lecture about survival skills. I couldn't help thinking how much nicer this might have been in July. Our instructor was a grizzly looking man called William who said he was an ex-marine. 'Do you know why you're here?' he barked when his lecture was over. None of us did but we were all a bit too scared to admit it. 'You're here to win,' he said, finally. 'Have you got what it takes?' Apparently not, because we were still too scared to reply. 'Well, if you're too pathetic to win for yourselves then you'd better win for me. Because my team isn't the losing team. This is what you're going to do.' He opened up another map and plotted out a course for us. It included stretches of ground wire we had to crawl under, water pipes we had to climb through, trees we had to climb and rope bridges we had to cross. 'You'll be racing against the clock as well as against each other. Now, I know you're just soft City people, but I'm not expecting anyone to give up. I'm not accepting any excuses about broken nails or dirty hair. Are you ready for this?' Suddenly I was. I hadn't liked the way he had looked at me when he mentioned the broken nails and the hair. If he thought I was going to fulfil some kind of stereotype, he was very much mistaken. There were ten of us in our team, six boys and four girls. I promised myself I'd end up in the top three.

We pinned numbers onto our backs and headed to the start of the course. The other teams were milling around with us. We would start, one at a time, in a randomly selected order. I got a call around the halfway point. 'Number eighteen. Go!' I dashed across the grass towards the first obstacle, a wooden three-bar fence. I threw myself at and over it. I stumbled as I headed towards the ground wire but I didn't fall. One of the other instructors was standing by the wires shouting instructions as I began to crawl, army-style, underneath them. 'Head down! Keep on moving! Use your elbows. Keep your head down. You're falling behind. Keep on moving!' The rest of the course passed in a blur, especially the hideous rope bridge. But I do remember the shock I got in the water pipe. I was convinced it couldn't be as bad, or as wet, as our instructor had told us. I thought the one he talked about would be for the army boys. He'd already called us City softies. I was sure we'd just do a shorter, drier version. We didn't. It was almost completely dark in the pipe. It was a long, downhill crawl. At the end you literally tumbled out into a freezing ditch and had to wade ten metres till the instructor there let you climb out. I'd broken all my nails by this point, I was totally soaked and my heart was racing. But was I in the top three?

'Number eighteen – good course!' The marshall at the end recorded my time and I joined the rest of the competitors in the changing room. Some people were almost crying. I felt euphoric. Mastering CDOs was one thing. Completing this course felt like an even bigger triumph. I found Sasha and compared notes. She reckoned she'd drunk about a pint of pipe water and she did look a little green. 'Do you fancy hunting down some traders?' I asked.

'I think I'd rather just sit near this bucket,' she said.

The instructors said they would announce the race results after lunch – sandwiches and plastic cups of tomato soup. Sasha perked up a bit when she spotted a group of guys she didn't recognise. They were all in their mid to late twenties, clearly worked out and had great clothes. 'I've never seen them before,' she said. 'Find out what they're talking about.' I headed towards them and listened in on their conversation. They were talking about rugby and they were all South African. That meant they were our IT guys. All our IT guys seemed to be rugby-loving South Africans. I sloped back to Sasha and she declared the place a trader-free zone. Then she threw up in the bucket.

She slept all the way back to London and I was pleased. I don't think I could have made small talk, even if I'd wanted to. William had read out our results just after we had eaten. It turned out I'd come fifth in our group of ten. I was the fastest girl and I'd beaten two of the six guys. But for some reason I still felt as if I'd failed.

Things picked up in time for Christmas. Sasha was right on the money about our party. It was extravagant. We had magicians, fire-eaters and acrobats entertaining us in a vast marquee somewhere near Moorgate. But once again, we were thwarted in our bid to join the brokers and the traders. In the City, employment apartheid was all the rage at party time. Each department had its own big bash. Ours was the middle office affair. While we ate canapés in our tent, the front office crew were being served a Marco Pierre White meal and listening to opera in the ballroom of a Park Lane hotel. The poor sods in the back office were probably reduced to a karaoke machine in Pizza Express.

The New Year brought insult to injury. Bonus season had begun and in those crazy, pre-crunch days – 2006 was notoriously lavish – the papers were full of stories about brokers collecting £20 million bonuses or dropping £45,000 on dinner at Pétrus or Le Pont de la Tour. Poor Tony had his ear bent almost every day in the canteen when I moaned about how bored I was and how desperate I was to move on up. 'This is the life I'm supposed to be leading,' I'd tell him, exasperated, as I pointed to yet another outrageous headline. 'Someone out there has got my life and left me with this one. It's all been a terrible mistake. We don't work in an office, we work in *The Office*. And we don't even have David Brent to take the piss out of.'

Jokes aside, I had decided to revive 'project trader'. I'd long since learned all I needed to about CDOs. I'd also realised that, in too many respects, my new job was worryingly similar to my old internship. Did anyone in the City do anything other than input numbers? Did anyone of us do anything that actually mattered? In those long, dark January days, I was so bored I wanted to scream. After four hours of number-crunching, I wanted to bash my face against my monitor. Then, when I spoke to the front office staff on the phone, I'd be shameless about joining them. 'I'll be your trading assistant, I'll fetch your coffees, I'll do anything – just get me out of this middle office hell,' I would beg. No surprise, perhaps, they never took me up on any of my offers. The mad girl who yelled at them from the middle office probably sounded a lot more trouble than she was worth. Desperation wasn't a good look, however hard it was to shake off.

I began networking again. I tried to persuade as many senior people in my bank as possible to see me. But very few could spare the time – or at least that's what their secretaries said. Just when I'd almost given up hope of getting through to anyone, I swang a coffee meeting with one fifty-something executive in charge of our fund management division. I laid my cards squarely on the table. 'I want to move out of my current role and do something more important for the company. I feel I have the right skill set to join the trading floor. I know I can succeed in a front office role and I just need someone to give me the chance to trade.' The man looked right back at me. 'You don't want to do any of that,' he said. 'Trading is no job for someone like you.' It was a near word-perfect repeat of the other two men I'd met. It fired me up even more this time. Someone like me? How dare this man assume to know what kind of person I am!

'But I've got all the right qualities for the role. I'm fast, I'm accurate, I've got good maths skills, good instincts, a real grounding in the back and middle office roles. I'm as determined as anyone. I'm ready to take it all on.'

The man decided to give me a history lesson. 'Forty years ago, no one with any self-respect went into the City', he began. 'It was comprised entirely of rich family stockbrokers and barrow boy dealers from Essex. The actual dealing was for thugs. It was just big men in rough trading pits where fights broke out every day. You know what I was told when I began my career? "Only shits go into the City", they said. That's the way it was then, and that's the way it is today. I have done very well in this environment, but it has not been easy. Trust me, no daughter of mine would follow my footsteps.'

'What about a son of yours?' I said, with attitude. 'Would you let a son of yours go into the City?'

There was a horrible silence. Clearly this man was not used to cross-examination. Especially from women.

'I think we've taken this conversation as far as it should go,' he said rising from his chair, his voice rich, tight, frustrated and angry. We didn't shake hands. I walked very slowly away from his office. His secretary, a large lady in her forties who had her hair tied up in a messy bun, gave me bit of a smile as I walked by. I wondered how she put up with him. 'Thank you.' I said.

'Good luck, my dear,' she replied. She must have been listening in. She must know how humiliated I felt. I slumped against the wall of the lift on my way back down to reality. I felt utterly exhausted, but at least I'd learned one more lesson. No man would help me get into the City. No man would let me join their club. I was walking a bit taller as I got out of the lift because I'd worked out my next move. It was time to ask the girls.

# Chapter 5

I DIDN'T HAVE THAT many City Girl role models, to be honest. Apart from the HR staff, all my bosses had been men. So I was thrilled when I was told we were getting a new, female supervisor, Michelle.

'Is there a traineeship scheme of any kind in this company? Are there any mentoring opportunities I could sign up to, even in my own time?' I asked at my quarterly appraisal. Michelle picked up a chocolate digestive biscuit as she considered her response. 'No,' she said, finally. 'As far as I'm aware, we don't run any schemes like that. I don't actually believe that anybody does. Would you like a biscuit?'

The internet saved me. I was researching trading jobs when I saw details of a 'Women in the City' support group. It promised fellowship, friendship and – most importantly of all – networking opportunities. I signed up and went to my first meeting. The evening event was being held in one of the ancient guildhalls near Barbican – ironic, really, as I think several of the guilds had refused to allow women to join for several generations. Walking in was surprisingly nerve-wracking. Sasha hadn't wanted to join me and my only other real friends in the City were Jason and Tony, who didn't feel like pitching up just to keep me company. I had rung up beforehand so I knew the exact running order for the evening. It began with forty-five minutes for drinks, which I decided to miss. Instead, I arrived just minutes before the key-note speech was due to begin. That way I thought I could simply take a seat in the audience, perhaps say a few words to the people near me, and ease into the whole experience.

It worked out pretty well. There were about fifty women there, most of them significantly older than me. They had all finished the small talk and the speech was about to begin, so I took a place near the low stage. A woman with a 'Harrods helmet' hairstyle that looked as if it could survive nuclear war, moved her bag for me and made me feel welcome. The speech itself was mesmerising. We were addressed by an equally well-coiffed and incredibly glamorous American woman from a Canary Wharf investment bank. She was about forty, the woman next to me whispered, and she had apparently taken home a four million-pound bonus the previous year and nearly as much every year for the past decade. She was a shining light, a beacon of femininity and style who also pulled in the big bucks. I thought she was fabulous.

Her topic was Current Perspectives on Risk Management. The subject was as dull as ditchwater, but she somehow made it interesting. She was clearly unimpressed by the way much of the City viewed risk at that point. She made it clear that if she were in charge,

71

it could all be done so much better. I couldn't, for the life of me, work out why she wouldn't be in charge. How could anyone else interview better than her? Surely she must be able to get any job she wanted. The audience all applauded after the talk and the question and answer session. Then we were guided back to the bar area for some serious mingling and networking.

At the bar I met a fabulously indiscreet City reporter from one of the weekend papers. She was pouring the champagne – for herself, as it turned out. 'There are more bottles over there,' were her first words to me as I approached in search of a drink. A few glasses of Krug later and we seemed to be the best of friends. Her name was Amanda, she was in her mid-thirties and was wearing a crumpled black suit over a tight, very low-cut peach top. It was immediately clear that she had an extraordinary contempt for the City and for the men who ran it. If my goal in life was to become a trader, it seemed that hers was to humiliate the people she was forced to write about.

'If you're at some fancy presentation in the City and some man comes up to you, holds out his hand and says he's the chief executive then let me tell you the correct response is not, "Nice to meet you." The correct response is, '"Dry white wine, please." These men think they rule the world. We all know they're screwing up the world. It's up to us to push them back in their box. Don't let them think they're bigger than you. Don't flatter them. Insult them. Though the real tragedy is that some of them will probably get off on it.'

Amanda then started telling me about a chief executive who had complained about one of her stories. Then, somehow, she changed tack and we got on to the subject of dating City Boys. 'Some of them are pretty cute, aren't they?' I ventured at first, a little tipsy on our free champagne. No surprise that my bitter new best friend did not agree. She was slurring her words, but her mind was focused as ever.

'When I see some great-looking twenty-something City guy in a business suit, I just think one word: arsehole,' she began.

'Come on, they're not all that bad,' I tried to say. Big mistake.

'Not that bad? Take away their fancy hair gel and they're nothing. The last thing they want is a girl with a brain. They won't date someone who will challenge them, question them or out-earn them. They only want relationships with women who will shut up. That's why they sleep with their secretaries. The poor girls get taken to some fancy hotel room the men put on expenses and they're expected to be so grateful and impressed. And let me tell you how it works. If they get back to their desks the next day in the same handmade Thomas Pink shirt then they're the office stud. If the poor secretary on £16,000 a year is in the same clothes, then she's history. She's humiliated, mocked, and might as well quit. You'd be better off dating a waiter, that's my advice. They've got more balls,' she said, tailing off as she took a very long look at the Italian-looking guy who had just taken up his position behind the bar.

I tried to move the conversation on from dating so I could finally get a few career tips. But by this point someone else had joined us. She was our age, a lot younger than most of the others there, and she seemed very happy to keep the old topic alive.

'You're new here, aren't you?' she asked when my journalist friend went off in search of more booze.

'It's my first meeting.'

'And are you new to working in the City?'

'I did a year of work experience and I've done ten months middle office work. I'm aiming to become a trader. That's why I'm here tonight.'

'Do you have a boyfriend?' she asked. I said no, not sure why this was relevant. I soon found out. Boyfriends were her favourite subject.

'Well, if you get a boyfriend before you get the job you want then you'll have to kiss your relationship goodbye,' she said with a worrying intensity. 'The better you do in the City, the less desirable you'll become. You'll be richer, you might feel better, you might have the cash to get even more beautiful. But you'll get dumped. City Boys think that women with important jobs will cheat on them. And how do they know this? Because as soon as they get big jobs they start cheating on their girlfriends and wives. It's the circle of life here. That's why us girls need to stick together.'

I looked around the room with a slightly desperate air. I was certain no one else was talking about men. I tried one more time to get the conversation back where I wanted it. 'But how can we get a big job in the first place? As far as I can tell, it's a closed shop. My company won't let me get close to the front office staff. It's like they need to breathe their own air. I want a chance to join them, but I don't even know where to go to get an interview.'

My new friend shrugged her well-dressed shoulders and when the journalist rejoined us, they went back to the old subject of feckless City Boys. I excused myself and headed to the Ladies. Hopefully I could talk to other people on my return. Dating advice was always useful. But I'd hoped to get something more concrete out of this evening.

As I came back into the main hall, the first person I saw was the woman who had given the presentation at the start of the night. I had imagined that she would be whisked off in some chauffeur-driven car immediately after the talk. I certainly hadn't expected to see her standing on her own. I rushed forward. 'Hi there, sorry to disturb you, but I just wanted to say your talk was incredibly inspirational. It's my first time here tonight and I really enjoyed it.'

I was given a wonderful, relaxed smile. 'Thank you so much,' she drawled in her gloriously languid accent. 'Where do you work now and what do you do?'

I liked how direct she was. I told her about my dreadful CDO job. Then I told her how much I wanted to prove myself by becoming a trader.

'Honey, you sound like I did a long time ago and I hope you're up for a fight. I've got to talk to some other people in a moment but before I go, do you want to know what I know?' She put her hand on my shoulder. She captivated me and of course I wanted to know what she knew. She smiled again. 'I know that if you're going to make it, you'll have to work ten times harder and be ten times smarter than the guys. You'll also have to get out of your comfort zone. The City doesn't look after its own. It doesn't rear its young. If you want to move up the food chain, you need to change banks. Once a year is good. More than that ain't necessarily bad. The City only wants you if someone else wants you. Learn the rules, honey, and you'll climb the pole.'

'Thank you,' was all I could think of to say. Then she gave me a wry, slightly tired smile, flashed some diamonds as she shook my hand, then moved across the room to scare the heck out of someone else.

The City doesn't rear its young. I both loved and feared that phrase. It gave me permission to jump ships as soon as something better came along. But it also made me worry I was already too old. How young is young in the City in 2006? Was twenty-five considered a fossil and had I missed the most lucrative boat in history? The meeting was breaking up and I decided not to rejoin my journalist friend and the surprisingly large group that was now gathered around her. I left the hall and headed towards the Tube. Along the way I walked past a breathtaking mix of buildings. There was some lovely stone work on the old, low-rise halls, then there was all the glass and steel exteriors of the brand-new office blocks that had been clasped between them. The City is always growing and evolving, and I became spellbound with the intoxicating architectural skyline, the kaleidoscope of old vs new on my walk home. I looked into the street to flag a taxi. As I did, the face of my 'trading is no job for a girl' man flashed into my head. If I have left it too late, then he's going to think he was right. Suddenly that thought bothered me more than anything else. From that moment on, a mental clock began ticking in my mind. I had a point to prove and I needed to do it soon.

I stayed up till 3 a.m., restless with my thoughts. I went online to try and find out about qualifications, graduate entry schemes, scholarship plans, the whole alphabet soup of professional associations and City clubs. I took notes, fired off emails and felt hopeful.

I'd wasted too long thinking that personal introductions or help from bosses could get me where I wanted to go. I had to go back to basics and sign on to some form of official apprenticeship. I became a world expert on the different investment banks and their fast tracks for traders. At work, Tony and Sasha said they would help me with the forms and make sure my 'statements of intent' and 'long-term career goals' were as sparkling as possible. By the time I faced my third quarterly review, I thought I was on the verge of making a breakthrough. But then I took my eye off the ball. I fell in love.

# Chapter 6

HE WAS A CITY Boy and I met him in a City bar. I was just about to send in the first of my trading scheme applications and I was out with a small gang of my CDO colleagues. We had picked a subterranean wine bar near the Lloyds Building. It was always a bit Frankie Goes to Hollywood 'Two Tribes' when we went out in the heart of the City. One gang of people in the bar would always be preening and pumped up and trying to impress another. Status meant everything, and people started measuring it the moment you arrived off the street. That particular night had started well for us. My group had somehow managed to commandeer a prime table in a booth. We were almost subliminally aware of another group who were outspending us by the bar. We could hardly compete with them on the money front so we decided we didn't like them – until one of the guys came over with a bottle of champagne and six glasses.

'We thought you looked thirsty,' he said. He was your standard-issue City Boy. Expensive suit, shirt and tie. Expensive hair. Expensive white teeth when he smiled.

'Thank you very much,' Sasha said, failing miserably to play it cool.

'We also thought you looked comfortable. What with all that spare space,' he said, raising his eyebrows and flashing the teeth one more time.

'Join us if you like,' Sasha said, just as he knew she would. It was a classic City trade. They had the cash, we had the real estate. We merged.

'I'm Seb,' he said. 'This is Richard, Ash and Alex.'

We introduced ourselves and the little comedy began. The boys had that classic City confidence. They clearly worked together ten or twelve hours a day, and knew each other backwards. They had nicknames, back-stories, anecdotes and jokes. All they seemed to want was an appreciative audience and we provided it. We laughed as one of them began telling a story, another interrupted, a third heckled, and the fourth finished off the tale. We laughed as they talked about other bars they drank in and girls they'd pulled. We laughed as they talked about restaurants, clubs, the best and the worst places to go in London. It was a seamless, totally natural performance and we washed it down with several more bottles of champagne. I caught the eye of someone on a table opposite when one of the fresh bottles arrived. Was that envy or contempt? I realised with a jolt that we were now the biggest-spending table in the bar. So this is how it feels to have money, I thought. How interesting.

Sasha and I escaped to the Ladies after about an hour. There was a queue and we whispered away at each other while we waited. 'They're all pretty full-on, but Seb's great,' she said. 'Do you think he's single?'

'No wedding ring. Not that that means anything.'

'Alex isn't wearing a ring either. And he's got his eye on you.' I felt myself flush. How mortifying for a twenty-five-year-old, self-styled City Girl. Alex was the quietest of the group. In the story-telling sessions he had always been the one who finished off the tale when all the jokes had been told. He looked about thirty, he had high cheek-bones, tiny dimples and long, wavy hair. He was just as bright as his friends, but when the spotlight wasn't on him he sank back into his chair a bit. In those moments he looked tired, as if he regretted how much time he spent in front of a computer. I wondered what he was really like. Take away the three amigos and I had a feeling he would be a very different character.

'How long should we stay?' Sasha and I were fighting our way through a sea of dark suits as we headed back to our table.

'Just till we get their phone numbers. Then we leave together,' she said, giggling.

The business cards were passed around one bottle later. The boys all worked for the same American invest-ment bank situated in Canary Wharf. 'So what are you doing out here in the real City? Have you been barred from everywhere on the Wharf?' someone asked when we looked at the cards.

'We're on the hunt for fresh meat,' Seb said unashamedly. I flashed a tiny look at Sasha. Don't go there, I wanted to say. She deserved better than that.

'We've been at a meeting in the Square Mile,' Alex said, clearly trying to close that conversation down.

I couldn't work out if his eyes were green or blue. But I liked them. I liked that he wanted to apologise on behalf of his friend. 'My mobile number's on my card. Send me a message, so I've got your number,' he whispered as our party broke up around ten-thirty. Mainstream City bars empty surprisingly early, probably a symptom of last trains and early starts.

'I think we know where we're going now, don't we, lads?' Seb had said as we all hit the streets. A lap-dance club, I imagined. My little gang slurred some last good-byes and headed off for tubes and taxis. God knows how much champagne we'd drunk.

Sasha was in a bad mood the following day. She didn't sit anywhere near me in the office but we met up for a chat in the coffee area. 'Why is everyone in the City a total bastard?' she asked just before lunch. 'They're just gorillas in nice suits. Fresh meat! How dare he call me fresh meat?'

I didn't say anything because I had a secret. Earlier that morning I'd got Alex's card out of my bag. I'd sent him a quick text to thank him for the champagne. He'd already replied and asked if I wanted to go out to dinner that night.

I waited till after lunch before I replied. I wanted a career, not a boyfriend. I wasn't Bridget Jones. I think I'd also subconsciously taken my journalist friend's advice and decided that I might be better off dating a waiter than a banker – or at least one of the cute bar boys in Corney & Barrow on Broadgate.

But I had to admit that the City was a lonely place. I didn't have any plans for that evening. The last thing I'd wanted was to spend another night trying to translate my flatmates' Gallic conversations and feeling like an outsider in my own home. I said yes to Alex and got ready to join him beside the Bank of England at six-thirty.

He had chosen the Conran restaurant perched high above the corner of Poultry and Queen Victoria Street. I'd read about it, but never had enough money to go before. It was a clear evening in early May, one of the warmest nights of the year so far. The restaurant had glorious rooftop gardens and before we sat down to eat we had a drink outside. We could look down on all the busy workers rushing towards the Tube entrances towards the suburbs and home.

After a while we moved back into the main dining area. Alex had ordered champagne without asking me. That seemed to be the City way. I've never quite decided whether or not I like it. 'I'm glad you texted me,' Alex said as we sat down.

'I thought at least one of us should say thank you for the night. We don't normally drink so well.'

'Well, I hope my colleagues didn't get too crude for you. We'd had a tough day so we might have forgotten our manners a bit.'

'We've all heard worse. So, how were the strippers?'

'What strippers?'

'Weren't you going on to a lap-dancing club? Tell me about it. I'm interested.'

Alex had the good grace to look bashful. 'We didn't go, in the end. But we do go sometimes and we would have done if we hadn't expected another big day ahead. I'll tell you about it another time, if you want. But not before we know each other a little better.'

A pretty young waitress had arrived to take our orders. It seemed obscenely complicated and expensive food, but when it arrived it was surprisingly simple and worth every penny. I felt as if I was on a film set that night. The most beautiful surroundings, culinary excellence and, of course, a handsome leading man.

Alex's eyes were green and speckled with grey, I realised. They were softer and kinder than I'd expected. As part of the group that did all the talking when we met, he was now ready to listen. He asked me about my background, my family, my move to London and my job. When I told him how bored I was inputting numbers and how much I wanted to be a trader, he was the first man *not* to roll his eyes or say it was no job for a girl. I loved him for that, long before I realised I loved him for many other things as well.

'I'd like to see you again. I'm very glad the boys and I muscled in on your table last night,' he said as he paid the bill with a jet-black credit card. I'd reached for my bag as the bill had arrived, trying not to think how high it might be. A subtle shake of his head was my signal to relax. The lesson was clear. The City Boy will pay. I let him, because for the first time this seemed to be because of good manners, not a desire to score a few points.

'I'd like to see you again as well,' I said.

We didn't kiss goodnight. But he hailed me a taxi in the street and told the driver to look after me. I was smiling broadly as I settled on to the back seat and heard my phone vibrate. It was a text. 'I should have kissed you' he had written.

'Next time.' I replied.

The City is pretty much the most utilitarian, least romantic place on earth. Even the architecture seems like a conspiracy against women. Don't get me started on the symbolism of the Gherkin and all those other big, phallic buildings. But over the next few weeks, Alex and I did find the City's softer side. We had some Parisian moments sharing a bottle of Bordeaux at tables on the cobbles of Bow Lane. We had cocktails gazing out into the night from the top floor bar at Tower 42. We headed south over London Bridge some Fridays and ate lunch amidst the famous food stalls of Borough Market, and we rounded off a tough day with a piano recital in a Wren church in Ludgate. Getting from place to place was an adventure as well. Alex lived in a penthouse flat in Bayswater and travelled to the City by motorbike. I loved the idea of commuting that way. I was so fed up with elbowing my way between Tube commuters twice a day. He had brought a spare helmet on our second date, just in case I fancied a ride. I did. He drove me down to the river near Chelsea Bridge and then onto my flat in South Kensington. Maybe it was a good way to get us up close and personal. I was terrified of falling off, so I held on to him incredibly tightly. It was a wonderful way to get to know each other, and to discover London.

Once, when we had dinner overlooking the Thames in Canary Wharf, Alex said he'd drunk too much to ride the bike so we headed back west on a river boat. Lights from the old wharfs and warehouses reflected off the riverboat splash as we sliced through the water, cuddling up on the airline style seats of the clipper. I couldn't believe that in nearly two years of London life, the only boat I'd been on was the bar boat near London Bridge – practically the only boat in the capital that never moved.

Alex also offered me inspiration. He was five years older than me and five years ahead of me on the City natter. He'd been brought straight into the charmed circle of a front office, analysing credit derivatives and other sectors on behalf of his firm's traders. He devised trading models, uncovered patterns and helped make everyone a lot of money – including himself.

After our first few dates, Alex started asking me to join him on nights out with his colleagues and friends, though not with 'fresh meat' Seb, curiously. Alex lived in a front office bubble. I'd not been paranoid when I'd imagined a City apartheid in the past. There were two distinct camps of City players. The first all seemed to have gone to the same schools – very posh and private. The second camp all seemed to come from the same county – Essex. One of my favourites from the former social set was a much older man called George. He was bald, overweight and pink. But he was still the one I wanted to sit next to at dinner.

George came from some ancient English family. 'I'm the professional black sheep in a long line of amateur black sheep,' he would say after a few too many ports. Then he would launch into a wild, endlessly detailed story about the eccentricities of his father, grandfather or great-great-grandfather. They would have made a huge fortune in a high-risk overseas enterprise, then lost it all in the South Sea bubble, to a calculating ingénue or at a roulette table. George, who was apparently making a fortune in Canary Wharf, was simultaneously handing it all over to a very happy wine merchant. 'I am the first professional drinker in a long line of amateur drinkers,' he would declare with elemental pride. All his stories seemed to begin with a declaration of some new professional status. Apart from being a born entertainer, he was the most impeccable dresser. At the end of a long, booze-fuelled evening he would remain immaculately turned-out, even as he stumbled in the street and steadied himself by grabbing a litter bin and launching himself towards a cab. I sometimes imagined him sleeping in pinstriped pyjamas. If his house burned down in the night, I don't think he would have left before putting on a tie, cufflinks and some handmade brogues.

The Essex boys were just as fun. One weekend, Alex raced me down to Brighton on his motorcycle while a group of colleagues showed off in hundred-thousand-pound cars they'd rented from some classic car association. We went to a greasy spoon café for Sunday lunch, spending a grand total of around five pounds per head. Two of the guys, both under thirty, were obsessed with the idea of buying a racehorse. We spent the day trying to think of the most obscene names in the Mike Hunt tradition.

Dating Alex brought me another benefit: it stopped me getting fed up with all the soul-destroying number-crunching at work. I was so busy planning nights out and coming up with ideas for weekends away that the hours at my desk flew by. Back in my internship, Jason had joked about me being brainwashed into submission and giving up on my dreams. Maybe being happy was the biggest brainwash of all. I stopped thinking about becoming a front office worker because in some ways, I felt I'd become one already. I socialised with those guys every night, I was in their gang by default. So, for the first time in my life, I let myself relax.

In those warm, lovely days not even Amanda, my cynical City journalist friend, could rain on my parade. We still met for the occasional boozy night out. They normally ended with her bursting into tears in a restaurant and needing help getting into a cab home. This time, though, she stayed sober for long enough to give her verdict on my relationship. 'It isn't going to work. It never does,' she said. 'Alex is not going to commit to you because he doesn't need to. City men are cavemen. They're genetically programmed to want as much sex as they can get from as many different people as possible. He's still in the preening stage with you. He's showing off his feathers like a peacock but it won't last.' I stopped returning her calls for a few weeks after this. I'm a positive person and I felt my life was going in the right direction. I didn't want to be held back by someone else's cynicism. Especially as Alex was about to do something extraordinary.

It was a Friday night in early August. We were back in the same rooftop restaurant where we'd had our first proper date. I was still amazed at how few women there were. Gay men who feel intimidated in local restaurants could do worse than head to the City for their dates. Two guys sharing a bottle of wine and talking late into the night don't stand out in the City. When men are talking about some secret project and leaning in close it really can look like courtship. Funny how a place so homophobic can also be so homoerotic. 'Look at those two over there,' I whispered to Alex as I nodded my head towards two very intense plotters. 'Do you dare me to go over and tell them to kiss and seal the deal?'

'No I don't. Because I want you to get out of here alive,' he said. 'Anyway, I've got something more important to talk about.' That's when he did it. Out of nowhere, he asked me to marry him. We had known each other for less than five months. The low noise of the restaurant receded to nothing in my mind. Everything was very still and wonderful. I said 'yes' without a moment's hesitation. Then I let out a very nervous laugh. 'Are you serious? You really want to get married?'

'I really do. You're the one, and there's no point in waiting. I would love to be married to you,' he said.

I looked across the table at Alex. He was so handsome, elegant and vulnerable in that moment. I almost fainted. Marriage was something I'd thought I'd do in my thirties. It was never supposed to come before my career. But this man was, indeed, Prince Charming. He was part of the City, but so different to the City. We complemented each other. I felt comfortable with him, yet inspired by him. I could prove my cynical friends wrong. You could get to know someone in five months. Whirlwind romances could last. So when I said 'yes' a second time I really meant it. This moment may not come around again. I wanted to be married to him and I didn't want to wait either.

'I don't think I want some big, fancy wedding,' I said the following day when we were heading out for a walk in Kensington Gardens. Everything still felt unreal.

'You don't want to wear the big white dress?'

'I can't think of anything worse. Does that make me unromantic?'

'It makes you even more special. So what kind of wedding do you want?'

'Something personal, private, really meaningful.'

'Well, let's do it next week.'

Amazingly enough, we did. Well, next month, anyway. We flew to my home state in America where Alex charmed my family and I shocked them by wanting such an impromptu wedding. When the day came, we left everyone else behind. We drove alone to the local courthouse in a rented Ford Mustang. I wore a black, knee-length dress, Alex wore a business suit and an open-necked shirt. We had no guests, just the court witnesses and officials. After we'd kissed and signed the register, we headed to a twenty-four-hour diner for pancakes and ice cream. Alex couldn't stop smiling and I couldn't stop giggling. I was also struggling to take my eyes off my engagement ring. He had given it to me a little late – less than an hour before the wedding ceremony, to be exact. But it was so worth the wait.

I'd opened the tiny ruby-red jewellery box in the town square. Inside was what looked like the biggest, most beautiful diamond in the world.

'How big do you think it is?' Alex had asked. I had no idea. I knew nothing about diamonds.

'It's 2.34 carats. It's D, the best colour as well,' he said proudly. I couldn't have cared less. It could have been blue paste for all I cared. It was beautiful. If only I'd known that one day, just two years later, I'd be blinded by tears as I tried to sell it at a London dealer. Maybe that diamond was jinxed. They do say that lots of the world's most precious stones are cursed. But while the going was good, I adored the way the light reflected in a prism of colours off the facets of my diamond. It was a thing of beauty as well as a symbol of love.

Back in London, I was less keen on the reaction my ring elicited from others. City Girls need to be very careful about the jewellery they wear. Pick a big rock, and the men who run your company may dismiss you as a trophy wife who's no longer hungry enough to do the best deals. I hate to say it, but the women who work alongside you react badly as well – simply due to jealousy. I saw less of Sasha after getting married, and I missed her. We never spoke about why we began to take lunch at different times. But something in the dynamics of our friendship had been broken.

Collect the numbers, input them here, check the totals, press send. Repeat and repeat all day. I slipped back easily into my old routine and I didn't actually mind it. Life was easy, all of a sudden. I had moved into Alex's flat in Bayswater and he dropped me off each morning on his bike before heading on to Canary Wharf. I was one of the first people in the office each morning and I had a strange sense of ownership about it. I'd walk between the desks when no one else was there, feeling oddly at home. I'm safe here, this will be enough for me, I said to myself. And it was, until two people burst my bubble and made me come to my senses.

The first of them was one of Alex's older colleagues. We had just finished dinner in a carnivore's paradise somewhere near the Barbican. It was long before the smoking ban, and the man next to me had lit up a cigar. It seemed there was no question that I might have objected. 'So what do you do?' he had asked. How funny that it had taken nearly three hours for him to ask me a single question.

'I work in the CDO division of another bank. I administer trades and work with the risk managers.'

My companion sucked on his cigar as he digested the information. He clearly felt the need to consider it from all angles. Then he gave a nod, like some kind of papal approval. 'That's a nice job for you to have,' he said. I flushed, though I doubt anyone could have seen it through the smoke. I interpreted his words to mean 'That's a nice job for Alex's wife to have.' A job that was small, dull and utterly unthreatening.

The next person to snap me out of my slumber was dear old Jason.

We were catching up for the first time in about five months. I'd bored him with a few wedding pictures and a description of my new favourite shops in Bayswater. I'd told him how happy I had become at work. That's when he said it. 'You've given up on "project trader", haven't you?'

The words stung – probably because they were true.

'Ten pounds says you'll be at home baking cakes and having babies by Christmas,' Jason continued.

I was appalled. 'I will not. I'm only twenty-five. I'm still going to make it.'

'But you just said you enjoy your job now. You said you've come to like it. Easy commute, nothing to get stressed about, plenty of time to organise the rest of your life. It sounds perfect.'

'Well, you know, it's not perfect for me.' I nearly had a panic attack later on that night. Jason and I had moved on to talk about other things, but I'd not been able to get his words out of my head. I kept hearing the American lady from my first female City meeting as well. She'd made me believe I was too old to get ahead back then. How many more months had I let slip now? How many bright young graduates might have leapfrogged me while I set up house with my husband? 'Jason, I'm so sorry but I've got a bit of a headache. Do you mind if we call it a night?'

We said subdued goodbyes on Fenchurch Street and I headed home to Bayswater. I don't know why, but I had a terrible feeling I might never see Jason again. We'd beaten the odds by staying in touch as long as we had. But our jokes were wearing a bit thin by now. We had ever fewer people in common to discuss. It was probably time to move on.

Alex could tell something was wrong the moment I got in. I made myself a cup of camomile tea and joined him on the sofa in the living room. 'Jason said something which I didn't like but which might actually be true,' I began haltingly. 'He sort of suggested that I've lost my way and given up on my dream of having a proper career. He thinks I'm going to become some sort of 1950s housewife. But I don't want to do that.'

'I don't want you to do it either. I don't think I really want a Stepford wife. Look, I'll never hold you back. You know that.'

I smiled at him and got close. He felt so right. Our honeymoon was over, but in the very best way. 'I've somehow let a whole year slip by in a job that drives me mad. But I'm going to start networking again,' I said quietly. 'I'm going to be in the front office by the end of the year.'

Amanda and I had got back in touch and she helped me out. She went through her contacts and set me up for breakfast with the managing director of one of the City's biggest European banks. 'If he can't find you a job then no one can. He's better connected than anyone else I know,' she said.

Our breakfast was set up for the Garden Room at the Savoy Hotel the following Tuesday. Alex was hugely impressed. 'That's a hardcore location. The Savoy is serious deal-making territory,' he said. 'If he's taking you there he's serious about you. I think this could be your moment. You're going to leave that place with a job offer in your pocket.' There was genuine excitement in his eyes that day. My triumph would be his triumph. I was an only child and it felt wonderful, all these years later, to have someone entirely on my side.

'I assume you want to know about my job,' Amanda's contact said, drinking black coffee out of a gorgeous, ivory-coloured cup.

'I want to know about working in your team, yes,' I said. He ignored me. 'I earn a basic salary of just

£200,000 a year, but I aim to collect a bonus upwards of £800,000. I lead a team of eight men and I'd be disappointed if they weren't getting four times their salary in bonuses in a good year. Our job is to make sure every year is a good year.'

Two perfect poached eggs on white toast with the crusts cut off had arrived. Rich yellow yoke poured out on to the plate as I cut into mine. My companion ate his very fast. He had more to say. 'On a personal level, I have four children, all in private school. They have a one full-time nanny for the week, one for the weekend. One of them joins us on all our holidays. We have a place in Vence, in the South of France, and a chalet in Verbier. Do you know Verbier?'

'I don't actually ski, but I have heard of Verbier, of course.'

'It's blue chip property. Ski in, ski out, recession proof. The Russians are pushing prices up to crazy levels. It's really quite amusing. It's the same in the South of France. A wooden shack with a tin roof can go for a million euros if the view's right. My view is superb.'

'And the team you have at the bank? How do you recruit them?'

He ignored the second of my questions. 'They work as hard as I do. They'll have been in for an hour by now. Maybe they'll have earned enough to buy a new Porsche each.' He laughed very loudly at that. I cringed in the hush of the Savoy dining room. This whole breakfast had been a nightmare. He hadn't asked a single question about me. He didn't seem to care who

I was or why I had wanted to meet him. Whenever I tried to interrupt or change the subject, he countered with another story of a deal he had done or a property he had bought.

He paid the bill with fanfare, then flashed me a huge smile. 'It has been an absolute pleasure, but I really must go,' he said.

I walked, dazed, to the Ladies. I'd got nothing out of that, but then neither had he. So what had been the point? It wasn't even 8 a.m. and I felt as if I'd been mugged, drugged or both. At midday, I decided to push myself forward one last time. I decided to call him, say I'd been deeply inspired by his example and wanted to work for him. His secretary refused to put me through. 'Does he know you?' she asked.

'No, he really doesn't,' I heard myself say, and hung up.

I stayed in a daze for the rest of the afternoon. That must be why I made my first and last big mistake.

Alex dropped me off at the Starbucks on Fenchurch Street as usual just after 7.45 a.m. the following morning. I went in to read the papers with my usual latte. This was always my favourite time of the day. I was in the City an hour earlier than I needed to be. It allowed me to relax and watch all the other people scurrying to their offices. I was City Girl, and I always felt calm and surprisingly free at this point. I loved the anonymity of my window seat, looking at the little patch of sun that sometimes edged between a gap in the buildings and reflected against the pavement in front of me.

Most mornings I clicked through security and headed to my desk just after 8.30 a.m. I liked being among the first to arrive. 'The calm before the storm of boredom' is how I described it to Alex. It was oddly reassuring.

That morning, however, there was something different. Late last night I'd been sent an email from Michelle saying she needed to see me as soon as possible in the morning. I'd never had a message like that before, not from Michelle, nor her predecessor. I looked across the floor. Her office door was open and her room was empty. I don't know how I knew it was bad news. Could someone have seen me in the Savoy yesterday? But even if they had, a power breakfast isn't a disciplinary offence. I'd still arrived pretty much on time. And it wasn't as if other people weren't looking for new jobs every day of the week.

Tony didn't catch my eye when he arrived and I greeted him. Oh God. He knows something. Does everyone? 'What's going on? I've got a message saying I need to see Michelle. Do you know what it's about?' I asked.

Tony gave a totally unconvincing shrug.

I spent the next hour tapping in my numbers as normal. Every few minutes I twisted in my chair to see if Michelle had arrived. I nearly had a heart attack when my phone rang. The single ring that said it was an internal call. Was it my imagination, or did Tony and the whole team tense up as well?

'Hello, Suzana speaking.' I said.

'Suzana, it's Michelle. We need to see you in the meeting room right away.'

That walk was the worst of my life so far. It was no more than a hundred metres. But it could hardly have felt more public. Everyone's heads were down, but everyone seemed to be watching me. What on earth had I done and how come everyone knew?

'Suzana, sit down. This is the head of our settlement department.'

I nodded a greeting and looked from this stranger back to Michelle. 'Has something happened?' I asked, desperate not to hear a crack in my voice.

It turned out that something had. I had somehow forgotten to tap in one figure the previous day. Because of that one error a trade hadn't been reconciled and we had been hit with a 700 euro late-payment fee.

'I am *so* sorry,' I said when Michelle had finished the explanation. 'I've never made a mistake or missed anything before. I really can't explain it. I'm sorry.'

'So are we,' said Michelle drily. 'That's why we're going to ask you to leave.'

Everything went very quiet and very slow. Leave for the day, or leave for good? I knew, without asking, that it was the latter. Looking back, I know I could have fought it. It couldn't possibly be legal to let someone go after a one-off mistake. Amazing, today, that City Boys keep their jobs and their bonuses after losing millions of pounds – and that in 2006 this City Girl was cast out after losing just 700 euros.

'We'd like you to leave today. This afternoon. Now, in fact,' Michelle said. I caught her eyes flash down to my left hand. Why was she looking at my engagement ring? It probably meant nothing. I certainly had no time to think about it. Banks are brutal when they want you out. I had to turn over my security pass in the meeting room. Then I had to walk back out to my desk.

Does everybody know? Are they laughing at me? I was mortified as I walked through the office. I tried to keep my eyes dry and my face impassive. I even managed to smile at Tony when I got back to our pod. 'I've been sacked,' I told him. 'For missing a trade yesterday and costing us a late-payment fee. They want me out right now.' Bless him, I'm sure Tony would have fought for me, if I'd have asked him to. But to my mind, I'd left the moment Michelle had asked me into that meeting room and closed the door. I sat down briefly and wondered if I needed to log off my computer or if some central department had already shut me out of the system. I didn't bother to find out.

Packing up didn't take long. I had one spare pair of shoes under my desk and one set of dry-cleaning on a hanger by the door. I had no family photos, no books, plants, personal items or files to remove. So I wouldn't be one of those tragic figures you see on the news walking out of office blocks carrying cardboard boxes full of crap. I just left with a tiny gym bag and a quick kiss with my immediate colleagues.

Down in the lobby, the electric gates slid shut behind me for the last time. In the street busy pinstriped people rushed past me, just as they had on my first day in the City less than two years ago. I headed towards the Tube, with no idea what to do next. I was twenty-five years old. I'd paid my dues in the capital's dullest jobs. I'd seen the way the City worked from the inside – and from the ground floor. I'd seen how each function fitted in with all the others and why every link in the chain had to be as strong as the next. I had swallowed my pride and networked in every way I knew. But they had still tried to spit me out of the system. Do I run away or do I fight? I was walking past a travel agency as I asked the question. I looked at the pictures of cruises and tropical beaches in the window. Then I looked at all the busy, successful people scurrying around me on the City pavements. It would be so easy to escape from all of this. But it would be wrong. This wasn't over. There was no way on earth I was going to let the City Boys think they had won.

# Chapter 7

THE MAN LOOKED UP from his notebook. 'Give me an example of a time you took a risk.'

'I married my husband after knowing him less than five months.'

'And has it worked out?'

'It's worked out perfectly. I never doubted that it was the right thing to do.'

It was also the right answer to this man's question. He put down his pen and smiled. 'When can you start?' he said.

Four days had gone by since I'd been booted out of my old job. Four days of frantic activity. I hadn't called Alex to say what had happened. He always said his company policy was that someone – in either his or my immediate family – had to have died before they put personal calls through during market hours. Instead, I'd gone home alone and cried alone. I'd punched the pillows of our bed alone. I'd screamed alone in our bathroom. Then I opened a bottle of very expensive wine, toasted my uncertain future and started cooking. 'This is a surprise. What's going on?' Alex had said when he arrived home just after seven.

'You're not going to believe it. Your wife is unemployed. I've turned into a 1950s housewife after all.'

'They made you redundant?' It sounded like a crazy question. It was 2006. Markets were still shooting up. House prices were still zipping ahead. The economy was buoyant. Why would anyone in the City ever get made redundant?

'No, I've been sacked. It was a silly mistake, but I'm fine about it. It was the kick up the backside I needed. I know I've said it a thousand times, but this time I mean it: as of now, I really am going straight to the top.'

Alex took the wine glass out of my hand. I admit there might have been a touch of hysteria in my voice and the kitchen knife at my side probably bothered him a little. I smiled at him reassuringly. 'I missed a trade. It was the most stupid administrative error in the book. It had no effect on anything whatsoever. They had to pay a late-payment fine and that's all. But one mistake turned out to be one mistake too many and they wanted me out. So I've got no job.'

'That's OK.'

'No, it's not OK. It's my wake-up call and I've done a lot of thinking today. No more pointless phone conversations with front office staff who don't even know who I am. No more meetings with men who aren't going to take me seriously. It's back up or shut up time. And I've already found a way in. This could all work out absolutely perfectly.'

I'd got lucky that afternoon when I'd been recipe-hunting online. I looked at all the usual recruitment

102

websites as well. Then I'd scouted around some of the less well-known banking sites. After an hour, I found something. One of the private firms was looking for graduates. You didn't need to be fresh out of college to apply. In fact, a bit of life or work experience was welcomed. I clicked to get more information. The job on offer wasn't for the faint-hearted. It was to be a pro- prietary trader – an intraday trader. That was one of the highest stress occupations in the city. Those traders almost literally live or die by their results each and every day. There was no hiding place for poor performers. No escape for people who didn't thrive under pressure. The website promised a very steep learning curve for successful appli- cants. The more I read, the more desperate I was to climb on to it. The most amazing thing happened when I clicked to read the application details. I had seen the advert in the nick of time. The bank took people on just once a year and the closing date for applications was in three days' time. A series of day-long interviews would begin shortly afterwards. I had never wanted anything so much in my life.

I had made it past the first stage and my first full inter- view day had begun at 9.30 a.m. I was in a Canary Wharf skyscraper with an HR officer who barely looked me in the eye. That was a bit annoying, really, as I'd spent eighty pounds in Harrods that morning having a breakfast-time blow-dry, manicure and professional make-up session in the fifth floor urban retreat. The HR person was a polished-looking dark-haired man of about thirty-five. He had to go through all the most basic information about who I was, where I was from, how I'd been educated, and if I'd ever been in prison, in rehab, or insolvent. I explained why I'd left my previous job and was thrilled when he waved it away as unimportant. I then spent an hour filling in forms with him before the real pressure began.

'The next stage is mathematical testing,' he said. 'I'll take you to the exam room.' I was led down a corridor and past some breathtaking art. There were five rows of four desks in what seemed to be a windowless room. Half the desks were occupied, and after I arrived a trickle of other candidates filled up the remainder. Where did they come from? Just how many HR men does this bank employ? I tried to stay calm as I sat down.

Amanda had advised me to keep looking around every new room for cameras. I couldn't see any but I kept my guard up. I didn't want to give away any clues about how nervous I felt inside.

'You have just five minutes and there are forty problems to solve. You don't have to complete them all, but clearly, the more you finish correctly, the more favourably your application will be viewed,' we were told. 'Your time starts now.'

I turned the page and began. Some were simple additions, subtractions and multiplications. Then there were some very lengthy long divisions, some fractions and some really complex stuff. Even before the examiner had given her little explanation, I think I'd guessed that this wasn't just about getting every single answer right. I soon spotted that it would be impossible to answer all of the questions in the allotted time. So they must be watching how we did the test, just as much as what we wrote down as the answers. On one level, they must have wanted to see how we coped with the competition – and some of us coped badly. I could see one poor guy to my left too freaked out about what he thought everyone else was doing to put pen to paper for about a minute.

On another level, I sensed that the real test was in our ability to manage our time. Traders need to know which fish to fry and which to throw back. We had to trust our gut instincts, moving past the questions that we knew would take too long or require too much effort to answer. I could sense several of my fellow interviewees bombing out, pondering over a tricky long division problem for a full minute only to find that time was up and they hadn't completed even half the test. I'm proud to say I breezed through all that. I seemed to know exactly which mathematical fights were worth having. I might not have answered every question, but I made it to the end, I didn't waste a second, and I didn't get any answers wrong. That's the examination equivalent of being 'in the black', or profitable. It's the only thing that matters in the City.

All twenty of us were then taken to a different but almost identical room. The session we faced at this stage seemed to be designed to test our sanity – ironic considering the number of crazies I would end up working alongside once I'd got the job. We had to stand up and say four different things about ourselves. Then we had to ask the person on our left a question, then ask the person on our right a different question. Every question had to be different as the focus moved around the room so things were getting a little light-hearted by the end.

That's when we got a shock. Talking in front of the group was only the first part of the test. Each of us then faced a question from the group leader to see how much information we had absorbed. 'Where was this candidate born? Which university did that candidate attend? How old is this candidate? Which of these four candidates admitted to being nervous?' The questions moved around the room and in one of two simple phrases – 'That is correct' 'That is incorrect' – we heard our fate. If I hadn't been so terrified, I might have stood up and congratulated them on how ingenious this was. Most of us only pay attention to our own words and only pretend to listen to others, especially when we're under pressure. I certainly was, because as one of the first to enter the room, I was sitting on the far right-hand side. That meant I was one of the last to get my question. All the easy ones would have been asked by the time she gets to me, I thought. I wondered if the hidden cameras could tell I was barely breathing. 'Tell me how many people here went to Cambridge University,' she said. Dozens of questions, answers and splintered conversations flew through my mind. A handful of key words and phrases somehow stuck. 'Three,' I said, on instinct alone. 'That is correct,' she said. I allowed myself to breathe again.

A lot of spirits had been broken by the time we left that room. But the most important interview was still to come. We were being seen individually, and I had been preparing myself for this moment all weekend. 'You know how they always tell you to be yourself?' Amanda had said over her usual bottle of white wine. 'Well don't be. Not in a City interview. They don't want someone nice. At this level, you don't need them to like you. It will be all about persuading them you can make money for them. They will be there solely to assess your potential profitability. They want a machine. In a lot of ways, the more human you are, the worse you'll do. It's going to feel totally bizarre. But this is the way to get in.'

Amanda might be the most cynical person I'd ever met, but I somehow knew she was right. I thought back to all the powerful men I had met in the City so far. With only a few minor exceptions, they all had the social skills of a plank of wood. There was the shameless boasting, the total obsession with money and winning, the utter lack of humility or self-awareness. All the characteristics I despised made them shoo-ins for the City. I decided that if they could act that way with a straight face, then so could I. I decided to conjure up my old City Girl persona: the cool, confident character I had taken on when I needed to escape the boredom of my first work-experience job. I'd loved pretending to be a powerful City woman back then. Now I had to do it for real.

I was ushered into a small, achingly bright room for my one-on-one session. The interviewer was a sour-faced, short-haired man who barely smiled when I said hello. I sat opposite him and took a deep breath.

'So, what drives you?' he asked as the opening question.

'Money,' I said, keeping my face totally deadpan. I'd decided to be direct and focused. I thought short, one-word answers would work. Time is money in the City, I told myself. No one wants to hear any waffle.

'And why do you want to be a trader?'

'Because I want to make a lot of money.'

'Who living or dead would you most like to meet and why?'

'Warren Buffett so I can get some investment tips.'

We carried on like this for a while and I could tell it was working. It didn't really matter what the question was. In the City 'money', or some variation upon the theme, was always the correct answer. Amanda was right that you didn't need to be nice.

I kept that in mind when we moved on to my outside interests. No way was I going to wax lyrical about helping the homeless at the weekend or trying to fight climate change. The correct answer, once again, runs something along the lines of: 'Outside interests? Why would I have any of those? All I want to do is make money.' Say that with a straight face and you're one step closer. Somehow I managed it. After a while, I was almost enjoying the game.

The next bit about my skills as a team player was interesting. The interviewer made it clear that these skills were important. It was obviously one of the areas where girls often lost the plot. If we've not been in the right house at our posh boarding school or played rugby for our university college then we won't have the right credentials, right? Wrong. In the City being a team player means just one thing – that you won't rock the boat and screw things up for anyone else. Pack mentality is all about chasing the money. As long as girls make it clear they're ready for that race, then they can get to the next stage. So the questions continued.

We moved on to some of the psychological questions that you read about in management books. I was never quite sure why people bother with these when no one ever says what they really think. My favourite came right at the start. 'You have come across a man on a bridge. He is trying to commit suicide because he has lost all his money. Which of the following four things would you to say to him to stop him from jumping?' I was handed a sheet of paper with my four choices. A: There's a lot of people who care about you. B: You haven't actually lost all your money. C: I can find you a new job. D: Go ahead and jump.

I dismissed A and C straight away. Even the most popular people in the world can commit suicide, and I thought a new job sounded like too much hard work for someone who was already vulnerable and broken. B looked like a good answer as it got right to the heart of the issue. But, really, wasn't it D? Do City workers really help other people? Helping others takes time. That was time you could use making cash for your bank or yourself. I decided you could wrap the answer up in a lot nicer, more palatable psychobabble. You could say that you were just hoping to call the man's bluff. That he was probably hoping for sympathy and if you don't give it he'll stick around till someone else does. You could say you're being cruel to be kind. Pitch it how you will. But I had a feeling in that interview room that in the City the answer will always be to screw the losers and move on. That's why I crossed my fingers under the table and said I'd tell the poor man to jump off the bridge.

When that tricky little question was out of the way, the interview became deliberately disorienting. The questions lurched from topic to topic. From my attitudes and goals to my past experience. From psychological exercises to current events. From financial statistics back to my education. It meant there was no way of knowing if we were at the beginning, middle or end of the process. When I left the room I found out I'd only been in there for forty minutes. It felt like several hours. Despite my short answers my throat was sore. Interestingly, the only glass of water in the room was in front of my interviewer.

'Tell me about the course you did at university,' he said at one point. I'd worried that my music degree might be a turn-off. Far from it. I know now that the City loves performers. The bosses like to know you're confident enough to do whatever it is you do in front of a crowd. They assume this means you'll be able to run your portfolio with panache. Athletes and sports people get the nod as well. The City likes the adrenaline, stamina and the competitive natures of athletes and musicians. The city life will reward their dedication, even if it destroys their physiques with too many hours at work, too much rich food and too many pharmaceutical temptations.

'I went through a series of auditions to get on to the course, I gave recitals to up to four hundred people in the university concert hall, I taught piano throughout my course to earn extra money and I played keyboards in some of the toughest venues in the town. I've played for bar mitzvahs, at karaoke bars, weddings, you name it.' It was my longest answer yet. Beat that, maths grads, I thought.

A few more scratches of the interviewer's pen and he asked me what turned out to be my final question. 'Give me an example of a time you took a risk.'

When I'd told him about my shotgun marriage, he really did ask when I could start. Then he put it in context: 'That was a joke, by the way. I have no idea whether or not you will be taken through to the next stage. My notes on you will be pulled together with the impressions of the other people you have met today, plus the results of your tests and examinations. Then a decision will be made. One way or the other, you will hear from us in five days' time.' He stood up and held out his hand. 'Someone will take you back down to reception. Thank you for your time.' I was dismissed. So how had I done?

The rest of the week passed in a nervous blur. I hated being out of work. I'd never hack it as a kept woman. I sat in coffee shops, read the newspapers and tried to relax. I couldn't. Everyone with a job seemed more fulfilled than me. Any wage was better than none. I'd have happily retrained as a barista while I waited for my verdict on the proprietary trading gig. Foolishly, I relived every moment of the interview day. Had I worn the right clothes? Did I talk enough, but not too much, with my fellow candidates? Should I have made a follow-up phone call to offer any more information? And was 'money' always the right answer in the City after all?

On Friday morning, right on cue, I discovered that it was. The man from Human Resources called at 9 a.m. I'd passed all the tests, I had the right stuff. I was finally going to make it into a front office role. They wanted me to start in two weeks.

I told Alex the news by text at 9.15 a.m. If he got in trouble for reading a text at work then I was prepared face down his critics. I could easily argue that this was more important than life or death. He replied straight-away. 'I'll be home as early as I can. I'll bring champagne,' he texted. I had planned to cook that evening but my mind was racing too much to focus on recipes. I decided to order us an Indian takeaway instead. So much for the glamorous world of high finance.

So do I celebrate or do I run away? That's what I asked myself all afternoon as I power-walked around Hyde Park trying to calm myself down. Maybe this was the one thing they never told you about your dreams coming true. They're normally the start of something, not the end. If I thought that getting this job had been hard, then I had a feeling that doing it would be a whole lot worse.

'To becoming a trader,' Alex said as we chinked glasses over our chicken tikka and naan breads. I smiled, still feeling just a little bit sick. I was signing up to a one-year programme. I would be trained up, expected to pass the official exams first time round and, if all went well, I would be trading within two months. I would be on a probationary scheme for the second half of the year, trading the firm's money like everyone else, but subject to strict limits and supervision. The basic pay was low but from the second half of the year on, the bonus potential would be sky-high. So would the pressure.

The madness began at 7 a.m. two Mondays later. I got to the bank's head office in Canary Wharf at six-thirty so I had enough time to clear security and try and bag my favourite back-to-the-window seat in the meeting room. I'd decided to wear a very dark navy tailored skirt with a fitted jacket and new shoes. However much they might hurt, new shoes always made me feel more confident.

Nineteen others were on the same programme, eighteen boys and one other wannabe City girl. I didn't recognise anyone from my interview day. No one was late, and after I was escorted upstairs I realised I'd nearly missed the seat I'd wanted. No surprise that there was a real intensity in the air. The sense of fear and fake cockiness was palpable.

I looked around the room and got my first shock. The guys all had the exact same look. They had clearly been selected to fit a tried and tested template. Every one was in his mid to late twenties, had anxious, furious eyes and looked street smart. Even the slightly overweight guy in the front row somehow looked lean. They were all wearing dark suits, dark shirts and darker ties. An awful lot of hair gel had been used that morning, not all of it wisely.

By contrast, my fellow City Girl and I could hardly have been more different. Her name was Lisa. She didn't seem to be making any effort to smile at the people around her, let alone to chat to anyone. She was very still and her eyes were fixed on the pad of paper on the table in front of her. Something about her body language set her aside from everyone else. This might be the nicest lady in the world, but she's a fish out of water, I thought. Why have they picked two such different girls? My stomach lurched as I remembered some psychological report I'd once read. It was based upon a theory that if two women turn up at a party wearing the same dress they hate it and feel miserable all night. If two men turn up at a party wearing the same clothes, they're thrilled because it proves they chose correctly and fit in. They then relax and enjoy the rest of the party. Was some sort of subtle sex war going on in our fourteenth-floor meeting room? By selecting guys who all looked, dressed and appeared to act alike, the bank had given them protection. They had safety in numbers and were more likely to survive. I don't think

I'm being paranoid to say my fellow City Girl and I were left exposed. 'The City is threatened by women. It lets a few of them in, but then it does whatever it can to push them out,' one of the guests had said at my latest 'Women in the City' meeting. I'd not believed it at the time. Suddenly, I wasn't so sure. Divide and rule could be one of its tactics. Keeping the girls off-balance could be one of its strategies.

In the coming weeks, I really felt as if Lisa and I were isolated and forced to play unnecessary mind games. The boys could all talk to anyone they chose at any time. It wasn't as easy for us. If we sat next to each other, then the others all noticed it. Did it suggest we needed support and couldn't hack it amidst the boys? If we had coffee together, did it suggest we were deliberately distancing ourselves from the group and plotting against the others? Perception is everything in the City. Appearance matters. Rumours flare up out of nowhere. Lisa and I never did prove to have much in common and she ultimately didn't last the year. But it would have been nice to get to know her without feeling that we were scrutinised every time we spoke.

Back to that first morning. I was still feeling my way around this upcoming barrier. I wasn't, in fact, sitting anywhere near Lisa. So the first people I spoke to were boys. 'Hi. I'm Suzana,' I said to the guy to my left as a few others around the room made similar introductions.

'I'm David, hello.' He was probably one of the best-looking in the group. He must have lived in the gym prior to joining us. It was tragic seeing his body gradually go to seed as the crazy hours and lifestyle took their toll over the rest of the year.

The guy on my right was named Tobias. He was Norwegian and genetics had somehow gifted him the brightest blue eyes I'd ever seen. He was the livewire of our group and I would really grow to like him. He was the one who fantasised the most about a James Bond-style future on the trading floor, a life of instant rewards, fast cars and faster women. That first morning, we were still strangers as well as competitors. And we were excited. We were going to be proprietary traders and that was the best game in town, right? Behind all the nerves, there was excitement and optimism. This was the real deal and we were the chosen. Nothing could possibly go wrong.

The HR guy brought us all down to earth. He took an hour to run through the dullest bits of corporate life – the fire drill and evacuation information, payroll department and so on. However dull it was, I tried to remember every word. If they planned to spring a test on us, I vowed to be ready. Meeting point after a fire? Out on the South Colonnade. Change your bank details? Go to the nineteenth floor. By the time we broke for coffee at 8 a.m., I was a mine of useless information. Annoyingly, we never did get tested on any of it.

David and I talked a little more during that fifteen-minute break. A man wheeled in a trolley with silver flasks of coffee and tea, bottled water, jugs of milk and two plates of those pink wafer biscuits you never see outside of offices or three-star hotels. Keeping us in the room for the coffee break raised the tension a little more. The people in charge really were pros. With no change of scene, we were left with nothing new to look at or talk about. All we could focus on was each other, and underlying all our small talk was a need to score points. We sized each other up, alley cats eyeing up the competition and storing up signs of weakness in case we needed them later. Across the boardroom, I saw Lisa cxcuse herself from her little group and escape, presumably to the toilets. I could have done that two-by-two loo thing that drives men mad. But these weren't guys I wanted to drive mad – at least, not yet – so I stayed where I was.

David was reliving some of the questions he had been asked in his interview. His take on the whole day seemed remarkably similar to mine. Piss off and jump, was pretty much his take on the man on the bridge. His eyes were sharp and as the moments passed he seemed to exude more and more confidence. He thinks he's already made it, I thought. He really did seems to think he was in the club already.

Lisa had just got back to the room by the time our next introductory talk began. A risk manager who looked about forty addressed us. He gave us an overview of the bank and its operations around the world. He threw figures at us: profit, turnover, gains, bonus percentages, all lovely, magnificent stuff. Then he explained where proprietary trading fitted into the bigger picture. He threw some other figures around, smaller than the former ones but still many multiples of my former salary or the salaries of anyone I had ever met. 'You guys are the next generation,' he said at the end of his slot. 'We call you the gimps. It doesn't stand for anything and I'd like you to see it as a term of endearment rather than something derogatory. We need people like you once a year, every year. The good news is that we will give you everything you need to succeed over the next twelve months. The bad news is that we will take a lot from you in return – more, in fact, than we have taken of anyone in the past. Good markets may not last. The City is getting tougher every year. Things that were allowed in past years will not be tolerated this year. You will not be leaving at three to go boozing in Canary Wharf bars. You will not be given an extra hour in the mornings and starting at eight. You will be in for seven alongside everyone else. There will be no long, leisurely lunches. You will be here very late, alongside the rest of the traders. Your training will be full-on, each and every day. You will be on a roller-coaster ride for the next twelve months and you will need strong stomachs to cope. Do you feel ready?'

We all nodded furiously. If someone had stood up and yelled, 'Sir, yes, sir!' army-style, I don't think anyone would have blinked. Even if it had been me.

'The final piece of good news is that you will be taught by the very best in the business. One of our finest ex-traders will be teaching you how to make money for us. His name is Charlie, and he will be here in a few minutes. You will end up seeing more of him than of your wives, girlfriends or anyone else in your life. He will be with you in a few moments so I suggest you compose yourselves and get ready to learn. Welcome to the City. As I said, this will be the first of many very long days.' He gave the barest of thin-lipped smiles and left. The gimps and I were silent for a few moments, before a few nervous, whispered conversations began around the boardroom table. Just how bad was this going to be?

That was when the office door opened again. A tall, dashing man strode in with the fortitude of an African lion. There was a slight frown on his face, as if the very act of entering a room was wasting his precious time. He checked his watch as he approached the front of the group. We would soon learn that he spent most of his life checking his watch. He looked like a royal marine – which was somehow fitting as joining the City seemed akin to joining the army. He had expensively cut blond hair and a strong, tanned face that was brought alive by the ice blue of his shirt and tie. His dark suit was clearly made-to-measure. His confidence was effortless – I've never seen a man so comfortable in his own skin. So this was Charlie.

# Chapter 8

'**B**EFORE I SAY ANYTHING, I have to warn you. Eight in ten of you will never become successful intraday traders. Several of you will not last the full year's training. Half of those who do make it through will still get sacked. This is the toughest job in the world. It is also the best,' he said as he walked to the front of the room. It was a pretty impressive way to say hello.

Without any further ado, or a proper introduction, he clicked off the room's lights and pressed a button that brought down the window blinds. A screen in front of us lit up. For some time Charlie's name was the only thing on it. 'We are going to hit the ground running because I don't like to waste anyone's time. You all have a great deal to learn. I'm going to start off by reciting the twelve rules you need to burn into your souls if you are to succeed as proprietary traders,' he said. It was impossible to see his eyes in the sudden darkness but you could sense when he was looking at you. There was something almost sexual in the way he prowled around the room as he talked, like a jungle cat. I had eighteen alpha males sitting around me and I'd say every one of them was turned on when Charlie began talking about the money. The testosterone levels were sky-high. Whatever else happened in the City, this never changed.

'The good trade is the hard trade. If it's easy to sell, don't. If it's easy to buy, don't. Never let a profit turn into a loss. Ride the wave, don't get hit by it. If something doesn't feel right, get out. Listen to the room, but don't trust your colleagues. They are not your friends. They will spread false rumours to make a profit. Think for yourself. Remember that the markets can remain illogical much longer than you or I can remain solvent. Remember too that all rules are meant to be broken. The trick is knowing when and how frequently to break them.'

The presentation went on and on and we all desperately tried to write the key points down. The rules came thick and fast. So did the warnings. 'Trading is a continuous feedback loop that hits you in the face every minute of the day as you know your financial gain is directly tied to your performance. The pressure will hit you, mentally and physically. You will learn a huge amount about the markets. You will learn even more about yourself. Some days you will hate your colleagues. Many days you will hate yourself. You will scream at the markets and at the world. You will be on the verge of tears. But if you are strong enough and good enough and fast enough you get through it, you will win.'

The lights clicked back on, the window blinds rose silently. The mid-morning sunshine sizzled across the desk towards Charlie. I couldn't believe it was only mid-morning. I felt like I'd been in that room for a week. The contrast between this and my previous jobs defied description. I'd wanted a proper challenge for a long time and I was finally in the right place.

'So that is trading. Those are my rules. They are the words I want you to lock into your heart and soul. I want you to mumble them in your sleep. I want your wife or girlfriend to end up knowing them as well as you do. I'm going to give you something to read now to reinforce those rules.' He handed out some files and for the next fifteen minutes we read them in silence. The packs ran through trading examples when Charlie's rules would work. Further examples revealed how much we could lose if we ignored them. After exactly fifteen minutes, Charlie called our attention back to the front.

'Now you've got more of that in your heads, I'm going to explain how you're going to make money. I'm going to tell you exactly what it means to be an intraday trader.' The blinds and the lights went down again. The sudden darkness made it feel as if our four-teenth-floor meeting room was somehow being plunged into some cellar. This really was a roller coaster. By hitting us with so much information, in such quick succession, we were given whiplash.

'As an intraday trader you will deal with more stress than you have ever imagined.' Charlie said. He clicked a button and the complicated, official definition for intraday trading appeared on the screen behind him. 'Don't write that down,' he said. He clicked the words away and put it all in much simpler terms. Basically it is when you buy and sell the same instruments – in our case, interest rate futures – in a single day. That's why time was so important to Charlie. That's why we would become obsessed with it as well.

'As long as you don't care about your blood pressure, or wrinkles, there are a whole lot of advantages to intraday trading,' he told us. We wouldn't have any overnight positions to worry about. As our trades had to be done between seven in the morning and six at night, there would be no overnight stressing about open positions. We might have terrible regrets. We might lie awake sweating or having nightmares over a loss we'd made. But it would be too late to do anything about it – except to vow to do better tomorrow. As intraday traders, we would make our own trades and concoct our own strategies. We would, in a sense, be self-employed. All that made the job perfect for independent thinkers and fast decision makers, Charlie said. You can't do the job if you need constant affirmation from others. You only thrive if you can make it on your own. As he spoke, I knew I ticked that particular box. The final advantage of intraday trading was the big one: the fact that it's so tremendously lucrative. Charlie said the best traders could take home up to fifty per cent of their profits, and for some, this meant close to half a million pounds per year. He threw more numbers around to show how the senior traders had done in recent weeks. In the room, testosterone levels spiked higher. This was why we were all there.

'Now the disadvantages.' Charlie had started to

prowl around the room again as he talked. He strode past us all, ensuring we couldn't relax for a moment. 'There are few downsides, but the ones that do exist are not exactly small,' he said. The first was the most obvious. Intraday trading is one of the riskiest games in town. Only the very best can consistently make money out of intraday trading, we were told. You can't hope for something to come up in the Far East overnight. You can't hope Europe gets you out of a hole in the morning. On the intraday desk, it's over when it's over. Your P&L, the bottom line, tells you if you're a winner or a loser. Our P&L, Charlie said, would become our obsession. Everyone would have to stand up and be counted on it. It would level the playing field, and there was nowhere to hide.

'Before we go any further I will tell you one more thing,' Charlie said as the blinds went up and the light flooded back into the room. 'I've read your files and I know a lot about you all. I know you are all clever. I know you are all perfectionists. I want to be sure, however, that you know what you are getting yourselves into. This is not, I repeat, *not* a glitzy or glamorous job. If any of you came here today with those kind of misconceptions then I suggest you leave immediately. Trust me when I say it will be less embarrassing for you to go now. Does anyone wish to leave?'

His eyes were a rich amber colour, and they locked on to each of us in turn. I felt adrenaline rush through me as he stared past my insecurities. I held his gaze because I was certainly there to fight. Getting on to this course was no longer enough for me. So what if eight in ten people didn't make money. So what if half the candidates were sacked. At the end of our year I vowed that the last man standing would be a girl.

'We'll take a fifteen-minute break now. I'll be back to show you the Sim,' Charlie said as he left the room. He didn't look back at us for a second. He never did.

'What's the Sim?' Tobias asked. I had no idea. But it sounded great.

I was about to excuse myself and head to the Ladies when Lisa beat me to it. Again. Damn. I wanted to follow, but for some reason I didn't want Charlie to see me talking to her. I wanted him to see me as one of the boys. So I held on and silently cursed myself for having had a second cup of coffee earlier on.

None of us noticed at the time, but Charlie returned precisely fifteen minutes after leaving the room. Fifteen minutes wasn't just a phrase to him, it was a guarantee. From now on, every second really would count.

The Sim was the Simulator. It was the computer programme that would rule our lives for the next six weeks. We moved out of the meeting room and into our training room. There were twenty desks lined up to face Charlie's white board and the two financial data monitors alongside it. Each desk had the standard computer equipment and on each hard drive was the larger than life Sim programme. It let us complete dummy trades with fictional amounts of money, using the same platforms real traders used.

Using the Sim was remarkably similar to playing a video game, so it was perfect for the boys, who were all genetically programmed for this stuff. For them, this was playtime and you could see the joy in their faces as Charlie explained the way it would all work. For Lisa and I, it was a little harder. I'd not exactly hung around in amusement arcades as a teenager and I wasn't a PlayStation freak. The other difference between myself and the boys was that I never saw money as a game, either. Maybe that's why I beat so many of them at it.

Charlie spent more than an hour talking us through the way the Sim worked that first morning. It was intense, but exhilarating. When the initial explanation ended, Charlie then played out a seemingly endless series of dummy trades on the display screen in the front of the room. He portrayed several likely scenarios, and we took notes of how the red and blue boxes flashed up and produced either untold riches or gut-wrenching losses. Charlie was so severe and passionate about trading that the dummy money didn't only seem real – it felt as if it was our own. From the very first day, I tried constantly to second-guess him. I wanted to out-smart him, beat him to a trade and spot a winning bet a millisecond ahead of him. I couldn't do it, of course. But there was such a thrill in the chase. Maybe it wasn't too late to get addicted to the adrenaline rush. Everyone probably thought the first thing I'd buy with my first bonus was ten pairs of Jimmy

Choos. Maybe I'd surprise them and buy a motorbike.

If David's wasn't the first stomach rumble, it was certainly the loudest. The thunderclap from my left was so sudden and so loud that I momentarily took my eyes off Charlie and looked at him. He was mortified. It seemed that lunch was still for wimps. Hunger for anything except money was clearly a weakness. Charlie evidently had no time for weaknesses. He ignored all the involuntary noises, and traded through till 2 p.m. We had been on the fourteenth floor for seven hours with just one break for coffee. We had obviously been wrong to turn up our noses at the pink wafer biscuits when we'd had the chance.

'So, position yourself here and that bags your biggest payout.' Charlie completed another successful trade. 'It's not enough for a Lamborghini, but it'll buy the wife a new Porsche. It's enough to put a kid through private school for four years. Two years if they board and you drive down the price. Now you finally get the chance to eat.'

We were directed three floors down to the company canteen. I'd been expecting something pretty lavish, just as I'd expected a fancy loo on my first day on work experience in 2004. Once again, I was disappointed. The room was clean and very modern. The menu wasn't. This most high-tech of banks was serving food right out of a private school from yesteryear. It was all toad-in-the-hole, roast beef and Yorkshire puddings and sponge puddings with custard.

That day we got our trays and huddled together in

an empty section of the room with strained faces and fake confidence. I could sense that we were riding a wave of bravado. We were all trying to pretend we expected it to be this full-on, that we'd had no problem coping with the flood of information, that we didn't feel as if we'd been punched in the stomach. We ate fast, trying to carbo-load as much energy as possible for the rest of the afternoon. The food, of course, was deliberately perfect for the task. We were all desperate to see who else was there, to check if we fit in, to make sure no one was staring as us. At one point I felt like laughing out loud. We were adults, not children, I wanted to say. This is a job. It's not the army, it's not a cult and, despite the sponge pudding, it's not a new school. I kept quiet, of course. Because there was always a chance I was wrong.

Back in our training room, Charlie wanted to go over everything he had told us so far. That included the twelve rules he told us to burn into our souls, and the key details of the first trades he had shown us. The pattern of repetition and random testing would keep us all on our toes in the coming weeks. Nothing was ever wasted with Charlie. Every phrase could one day become leverage, edging you ahead of your peers. Fail to understand even the simplest message and you could fall short. I was mentally exhausted by the end of most days, but I would die before I showed it.

On that first day, 3 p.m. became 4 p.m. became five. Charlie didn't flag for a moment. If the word messianic had a human face, then it would have looked a lot like his. When he clicked off his computer after showing us more trades, I allowed myself to think the day might be over. But Charlie had other plans. He wanted to go back over everything again. He wanted to know how much we had understood and reflected on. With Charlie, there was always time to check things. Everything could be turned into a lesson for the future, and we must never forget anything. Only as our eleventh hour approached did he finally call it a day.

'Back here and ready to go at 7 a.m. sharp tomorrow,' he said. 'And if you think it's been tough today then you'll want to get a lot of sleep tonight. We move up a gear on day two. Do not go out and celebrate your survival this evening. I guarantee tomorrow won't be a good day to have a hangover.'

I was exhausted but fizzing with excitement when I finally got back to our flat. Alex rode the bike back from Canary Wharf as usual, so I'd taken the Jubilee and Central Lines. I was desperate to spot someone I knew – or more specifically, someone who'd never believed in me. I wanted them to ask where I'd been so I could pause for effect, then tell them I was a trader. Predictably, I saw no one.

'So, how was it?' Alex was there with champagne again as I kicked off my shoes. Surely Charlie wouldn't object to me having a quick glass?

'It was incredible. Terrifying. Exhausting.'

'I hope you mean all that in a good way.'

'I do, actually. I was really pushed and I can't tell you how good that felt. For the first time since university, I felt challenged, inspired and excited. I have no idea if I'll be able to handle the pace, but it's going to be a hell of a ride. All the way home I've been thinking of where I was two weeks ago. I was in crappy middle office, doing absolutely nothing and going nowhere. I was dry as a bone, bored out of my mind and wasting my life. Everything's changed. Everything.'

'You know, I don't think I've ever seen you look so positive. It's brilliant, babe. And what were the people like?'

It was my turn to smile. 'I've not really got a feel for the others yet. We're all too tense to really show our cards. But oh God, Alex, the instructor we've been given is amazing. He's called Charlie. He's awesome. He's seen everything. He's got more energy than anyone I've known. He's been doing the job for years and years. He's terrifying, but if he wanted me to walk over fire I think I'd do it.'

'Maybe you should divorce me and marry him.'

'If you don't run me a bath I just might.'

\* \* \*

When I'd calmed down a bit, I talked Alex through the events of the day in more detail. We drank the whole bottle of champagne (sorry, Charlie) and I tried to pass on every memory I had of the experience. I think I even managed to recite Charlie's twelve golden rules of investment. That night I slept the sleep of the dead. My mind was racing when my head hit the pillow. But the next moment, I was out like a light. I didn't dream – and when my alarm went off at five-thirty in the morning, I did something extraordinary. I practically leaped out of bed. It was the same feeling you have on holiday when you're desperate to get on out there and see things. In all my previous jobs, I fought to get up in the morning for my leisurely 9 a.m. start as I hid deep under the covers fearing the dispiriting day ahead. Now I was facing the unknown and seemed to have all the energy in the world. Charlie had said that the second day would bring a step change. Bring it on, I said to myself as I drank my latte and made myself look as sharp and City as possible.

The whole group was, of course, on time for Charlie's 7 a.m. arrival. He was wearing a sparkling white cotton shirt today and a ruby red Hermès tie. In our first six months I don't think I ever saw him wear the same tie twice. He seemed to change his watches almost as often. Forget the cliché about girls being obsessed by shoes or jewellery, City Boys can give them a run for their money with their own obscene accessory collections. Charlie probably spent more on silver cufflinks each year than your average family spent on food.

The first lesson was that there would be no easing into the day. No one eases into the markets, Charlie barked. In previous years, other mentors had given the gimps free rides and later starts. Charlie would not grant us that luxury as the markets were tougher and that was not his style. He expected us to be on our toes, fully alert, from the word Go. He also expected us to dress the part each day. He would police our fashion choices as thoroughly as he policed every other detail of our lives. It was suits for all of us, ties for the boys. 'When you make us a million pounds a year you can wear jeans or whatever the hell you want,' Charlie said. 'You'll see some crazy outfits on the floor but you'd better know that those guys have proved themselves. At the moment you're nobodies, so you'll wear what I tell you.'

After that warning, day two began with nearly an hour of the repetition and random testing routine. We were bombarded with questions about the markets every day for the next six weeks. The results were never recorded, but every day each one of us kept score.

When we broke for coffee, I chatted to Lisa for the first time. She was standing listlessly in front of the mirrors in the Ladies. 'It's pretty full-on stuff, isn't it?' I said, checking all the cubicles were empty. Lisa didn't really respond. 'Are you OK?' I asked, suddenly concerned.

'I'm fine, thank you,' she said flatly. Then she rushed for the exit. I took her place in front of the mirror. So much for me worrying about being seen as being too close to her. She must have already decided that the office was no place to make a friend. If I wanted one of those, I'd have to look amongst the boys.

Back in the training room, it was public humiliation time again and the echoes of boys' public schools seemed ever louder. One at a time we were called up to the front to perform trades on Charlie's Sim. Our moves were displayed on the projector for everyone to see. If we made losses, they were public. If we made profits, they were never quite large enough. Charlie's standards were extremely high. When the last of us had sat down again, he tried to explain why some of us had made erroneous trades. Then he gave us yet another caution. 'By now you should be able to see that this is not a test of maths. It's not a question of logic. If you're looking for those things then you have stumbled into the wrong Canary Wharf office block. This is about whether or not you can control what is up here,' he said, tapping his head. 'Stock markets are mirrors of the human psyche. If you can't control your emotions, you won't be able to control your profit and loss. And trust me, as this gets more serious, all I give a damn about will be your profit and loss. Over the next few months you may have your dog die, or your girlfriend break up with you. I'll only care if it affects what you do on my floor with this company's money. When you're in my group then your reputation is my reputation and that, quite frankly, is sacrosanct. Are you all getting this?'

We were getting it loud and clear. It felt like another army-style, 'Sir, yes, sir!' moment but once again we just about kept that in check.

'Good. Now it's time to turn on your computers.'

The room came alive when all our screens fired up for the first time. Charlie told us how much money we had been allocated as a virtual float. Then he gave us two hours to trade. And then he laughed at us – yet another way to keep us off-balance and on our toes. 'I don't give a shit how you did on those trades. If you lost money then you got lucky – just this one time you got away with it. If you did well and you expect some praise then forget it. I wasn't paying attention. But I will be next time. Now, grab some lunch and be back at two-thirty on the nose.'

When we got back to our training room, there were big stacks of books and papers on each desk. They were our Eurex study packs. 'You have exams in six weeks' time,' Charlie said. 'You need to pass these exams to be approved to trade live on the exchange. But you won't all pass. There are always a couple of casualties. If you're one of them you will be either kicked back into the Sim room, or worse, out of the company. So I suggest you pay attention.'

He spent the rest of the day talking us through the revision schedule. After the fireworks of his earlier presentations, this seemed much more placid. There were times when the rules and requirements he listed were mind-numbingly dull. But he still had us. He'd inspired us, fired us up and made all of us desperate to get to the next stage. Failing the exam? Becoming a casualty? I looked around the room sometimes. David could fail, or the wild-eyed Tobias, or even Lisa, my one fellow City Girl. But I couldn't. I wouldn't.

I studied ferociously, carrying my revision sheets almost everywhere I went for the next six weeks. In Canary Wharf I'd sometimes sit alone at lunch, rereading some tedious fact I'd already memorised a hundred times. At home, I had Alex quiz me almost every night for a month, on everything from option trading strategies to exchange opening hours. I took my materials to the pub or restaurants at weekends. In retrospect, this seems tragically sad. Yet at the time, it was exciting. I had my mission, to get out of the training room and to infiltrate the trading floor. Alex was my partner-in-crime. He helped me crack the terminology, understand the strategies and learn the regulations that we would naturally ignore once we had real money to trade.

The pace didn't let up as weeks past. We were at our desks at seven each morning. Charlie wouldn't accept lateness. He couldn't care less what London borough we came in from, or how bad the Tube or traffic might have been some mornings. If he was there, then we should be too. And he was always there. At this stage, we spent half our days working the Sim, perfecting our trading techniques, and the other half studying exam material. Sometimes external market experts came in to give lectures on different trading tools, on market patterns, financial strategies and other topics. It was a foreign language – doji patterns, Fibonacci retracements, candlesticks, butterflies, seagulls and all sorts of other strange terms that were to be found within the City dictionary. And if any of them could be useful just once, then we should know about them. We were voracious pupils. Charlie had been extremely clever pitching us one against the other. He had made sure we never forgot the intensity of the competition as we learned how to graph the spread on our screens, how to design charting systems and get the information we might need to cope with volatile market conditions.

Under this kind of intensity, we had begun to bond a bit as a group. Most days we stuck together in the canteen, gimps whom no one else bothered to acknowledge. A couple of evenings a week, at least a few of us would go to one of the Canary Wharf bars for a few drinks as well. Lisa rarely made it, but almost everyone else seemed to relish the chance to chat. We were rivals, not friends and we wanted to get information from each other, rather than give any of ourselves. But it all helped anchor us to the job and helped us to feel more at home in the City.

'How much do you think Charlie makes?' was one of our favourite topics. Rumours painted him as a legendary trader back in the day, when he played the markets full time. We heard stories of two million-pound bonuses and vast property portfolios across London and the home counties. He still traded a little

– but not much. Our training room was one level below the main trading floor but it was permanently wired to it. We could hear announcements constantly about important figures or economic results all day. Sometimes a random economic announcement would cause Charlie to freeze mid-sentence, dash out of the room and down to the trading floor to check on the senior traders. Ten, maybe fifteen minutes later, he would be back in our training room as if nothing had happened. He would pick up exactly where he had left off, almost to the word. There was no apology or explanation for the interlude. His poker face, as ever, was impossible to read, though naturally, we were desperate to do just that. We speculated endlessly. Our hero-worship was getting out of control. And the more harshly he treated us, the more we seemed to like him.

'Do you know that last year's group of gimps had a cinema club?' Tobias announced one evening. He had charmed one of the secretaries from upstairs, a good source for us to learn what was really going on in the rest of the company. Four weeks later, no one else in the building seemed to even acknowledge that we were there.

'What kind of cinema club?'

'They got off early every Wednesday and they went to see a fucking matinée. They never started before nine and Alice says they used to go boozing in Smollensky's at three every day as well.' That shut us up. We hadn't been allowed out of the building before 4 p.m. once. We were still expected to be at our desk every morning at seven. But after a few moments of hating Charlie for being so hard on us, we ended up respecting him all the more. One day we talked about asking him to join us for drinks that night. But after a brief discussion we decided it wouldn't work. It would break the vital hierarchy of the firm. That's why the senior traders sat at the best tables and never made eye contact. We were the gimps, so we were left standing by the bar, buying our own drinks and fighting for floor space with all the middle and back office staff. The idea of Charlie boozing with us was too preposterous to consider seriously.

In the early days, our other anti-hero was our big boss, a mysterious foreign billionaire who owned the company. One press report called him a recluse, but according to Charlie, he didn't exactly hide away at home. Instead, he came to work before everyone each morning, and left after everyone else at night. He had a colossal corner office on the main trading floor full of Ligne Roset chairs, we were told. Never once did he stoop to leave it and welcome us to his company. 'If you pass your exams, you might just get to meet him,' Charlie had said one day when the big man had walked down the hallway outside our training room. His message was clear: until we were official traders, we weren't even worth two minutes of the billionaire's time. Why waste your breath on someone who might not last the month? Until we could make money for him there was no reason for him to acknowledge that we were in his postcode. We were as replaceable and expendable as the bins.

Like most girls, I was brought up to have good manners. It seemed strangely liberating to realise that in the City – or at least, in proprietary trading – you don't have to be nice. You just do your job and get on with it. As long as you make money, diplomacy is a side dish. Eventually, I'd learn that the more money people made, the more severe they became. As would I – but that's another story.

'How much were you up today?' When we weren't talking about Charlie or the boss on our nights out, the gimps and I discussed money – in particular, what we'd do with our first-year bonus. The boys were obsessed with expensive gadgets. They loved talking about what they would buy. Martin, a short, sleek guy from somewhere in the Midlands, was the most nakedly ambitious of all. Right at the start he said he wanted to buy a Lamborghini with personalised plates. 'I want to get 100k, 200k or 500k, something that just says *money*,' he said.

'Are those plates available?' someone asked.

'I don't care. If you make enough money everything's available,' he said.

The other boys talked about planes, yachts and Swedish models. 'You know what Madonna said about toys like that?' I said once. 'If you can fly it, float it or you-know-what it, then you should rent, not buy. That's sound financial advice from a woman who knows.' The boys thought about it for a while. Then we had a long conversation about the cost-effectiveness of renting prostitutes.

Back in our training room Charlie gradually increased the size of our virtual trading clips. Or at least, he did for those of us who had been trading well from the start. I loved trading, even if it was just virtual money. When I made my first £1,000 I felt vindicated. Then I made more. Some days I made £5,000, some days £10,000, some days £15,000. I can't explain the buzz you get from that kind of result. The result of each day was boiled down into one key number: our profit and loss. In our world, that number was everything. Your entire worth as an employee, and as a person, was found in that figure. The good and bad thing about this was that it was an impartial measurement of your performance relative to your peers. Never has competition been so cruelly efficient or addicting. Like a drug, you always need a bigger fix. The amount that once made you happy always becomes your new benchmark. I was thrilled when I made my first £5,000. Then I needed a virtual profit of £10,000 to feel high. Then £20,000. It's insidious and deliberate. The City feeds you this need to out-perform everyone and leave them in your wake. Equally amazing, we felt this drive with virtual money on our Sim. If this was the rush we could expect with virtual money under fake market conditions, what would be the rush – and the pressure – when we finally did for real?

Intraday trading is unique. There's a world of difference between the type of fly-by-the-seat-of-your-pants day trading we were doing and the highly mathematical esoteric, model-based trading that was going on at the City's major investment houses. 'Pattern Day Traders', as defined by the Securities and Exchange Commission (SEC), was a term used to describe a trader who executes four or more round-trip day trades in five business days, provided those day trades are more than six per cent of the customer's total trading activity for that same five-day period. In simple terms, intraday trading is nothing but buying and selling stocks on the same day. This is done to take advantage of price movements and fluctuations that exist in the market. Traders are required to hold a daily minimum equity of at least $25,000 (an amount generously supported by the bank for us gimps).

The question I didn't ask myself, let alone try to answer, was how it would feel to lose. One of our guest speakers had tried to prepare us for the horrors of seeing everything go against us. 'If investment banking is the road to milk and honey, then intraday trading is the descent into darkness,' he said glibly. We didn't take him too seriously at the time. I'd ignored the white, shamed faces of my fellow gimps when they had terrible days. So far I had survived trading without crashing and burning myself, and I loved it. Quite simply, five weeks into my new life, I was still on a high. Every day was exhausting, but I felt so alive. The City had never exactly welcomed me. But now I was enveloped in it. I thrived on the market data. The immediacy, the excitement and the tension felt real enough in our training room. We knew how much more intense they would be when we passed our exams, and went to join the senior traders.

Perhaps it was hubris, but I felt my confidence increase with every trade. I wasn't even immune to the mental shopping sprees that the boys concocted at our after-work drinking sessions. I started to think of the gorgeous shoes I could buy if I passed my exams and started to trade. I thought about the exact shops where I would buy them – mostly in Milan. Previously unattainable material goods were now within my reach. As long as I held my nerve, they would be mine. And yes, there were downsides. I saw a lot less of Alex as I continued working long days and regularly socialising with the other gimps. I was too busy studying to keep up with many other friends, and I even struggled to remember to ring my family during evenings or weekends. But I was content in my City bubble, and I knew the stress would be temporary. All I needed to do was pass my exam. Then my life as a City Girl could begin.

# Chapter 9

THE EXAMINATION DAY BEGAN at seven – just like any other day. I was wearing my trusty Armani suit, my equivalent of lucky pants, and had been at Starbucks from six-fifteen, pretending to drink coffee but really just trying to clear my mind. I had twenty-five years of life experience behind me. But all that mattered was what I'd revised over the past six weeks. Life before Charlie was irrelevant. Sometimes I could barely remember it.

'All present and on time. Good. So how is everyone feeling?'

Charlie was in front of us at a minute past seven, like clockwork. He looked slightly pale, which was odd. I did a slight double take when I checked out his tie. It looked to be from Tie Rack. He caught me staring at it in horror and raised one slightly questioning eyebrow. I tried to give him a winning smile. It may have got lost in translation.

We were being examined in the Eurex headquarters in Canary Wharf, just a short walk from our offices. We were escorted into a large room full of computers, and a test administrator appeared to monitor the exam.

Amazingly, every one of us gimps achieved the seventy per cent level required to gain admission to the Exchange. Were we the new genius group of super-traders? Perhaps. But had you been in the room with us twenty, palm-sweaty hopefuls that day, you might have thought otherwise.

The exam format was no surprise – we'd seen these questions a hundred times before. The administrator's instructions swirled around our heads. Then he added one last instruction before we hit the point of no return.

'You can start the examination now.' The first set of questions flashed up on my screen and suddenly everything felt OK. I remembered how I felt at uni. I always liked it when the clock began. I liked it, just me vs the exam paper or computer screen. It was as if a competitive spark lit inside me, the very same spark that got me through the maths test two months earlier. Check off each answer, move to the next, keep it moving, Suzana. I liked being railroaded through this kind of assessment. I liked having something to prove.

I clicked my way through the early screens. I breezed through the section on options strategies, and was making good time before the final few screens on Eurex regulations. Less than fifteen minutes to go. Everything was fine and as the finish line came into view, I became aware of my surroundings. Our administrator was prowling the room, zigging and zagging between our desks.

Finally we escaped the building at lunchtime. For the first time in six weeks, we were all eating together

– and it wasn't in the miserable staff canteen. We had picked one of the illustrious American-style diners inside the ever-expanding Canary Wharf tunnels. It wasn't fancy, but it had big enough tables for the group. Simply being able to leave the office in the middle of the day and take our eyes off the market was invigorating.

I was famished, as my body reacted to the stress of the exam. I'd barely eaten the night before and hadn't been able to face breakfast. I ordered a chicken salad and devoured it like a wolf.

'We should drink to Charlie,' Tobias suggested towards the end of the meal. Everyone smiled as, we leant down the table to chink our glasses.

I tried to remember how many gimps had been booted off the course at this point in previous years, according to Charlie. It wasn't the most stable of professions I'd chosen. But the roller coaster had just begun.

'So, shall we drink to your success?' The wine had just arrived as Alex and I sat down for dinner in Notting Hill, and I gazed at him across an elegant, candle-lit table. He was so handsome. I'd seen so little of him over the past six weeks. I wondered, suddenly, how much he'd minded my absence.

'Let's just drink to us,' I said. 'And to life being a bit less chaotic from now on.'

'To us. And to many more lovely afternoons off.'

Charlie had sent us all home early when we passed, so I'd decided to fake a 'life and death' situation and text Alex. For once it seemed he was able to take a bit of personal time so he called me straight back. Better still, his boss actually let him take the rest of the afternoon off – unheard of in the City back them.

'If I make it this year, work will be more stressful, but with the exams out of the way, at least we'll have evenings together,' I declared. 'My weekends will be totally free. It's going to be great.'

'With a filthy rich trader wife, I'll be able to take things easier myself. I might consider becoming a kept man. A househusband. What do you say?'

'I don't think you'd last five minutes.'

There had been no casualties, to Charlie's absolute delight, and all twenty of us were admitted as traders to the Eurex Exchange in late 2006. That was a first for the bank. We celebrated with bear hugs, high-fives and a whole lot of macho air-punching.

That morning something else happened. One of the senior traders acknowledged us in the canteen during our coffee break. He didn't actually speak. To be honest, he didn't even smile. But he nodded to us as he walked in, and then nodded again as he left. No one had done that before. We were like giddy teenagers who'd just seen their pop idol. How funny that such tiny things can make such a big difference to the way you feel. I relished that sense of belonging – though it would turn out to be fleeting.

Charlie brought us all back down to earth straight after our coffee break. We were confused about being called back into the Sim room. Why were we still there? We're qualified, right? So when did we get to trade live?

'Turn on the Sim,' Charlie said. We were cocky enough to groan out loud. Charlie ignored us. 'Does it all feel familiar?' he asked. 'You reckon you've got to grips with it after six weeks? Confident now you've passed some big exam? You know what to do when you get out on to the floor?'

'Yes!' we chorused. Though it was clear these had been trick questions.

'I've got bad news. The Sim is just a game. Worse than that, it's a game with flaws. It recreates the market the way we might like it to be. However, if it was ever like that in the real world, then it isn't that way now. Hedge funds and automated trading systems have started to distort everything. The Sim doesn't replicate the way these investors affect your trading environment. It can't prepare you for the reality of investing today. If you're good now, you'll need to be that much better when you get out there and see that none of your little classroom theories can match the real challenges. Don't be complacent and don't think you've learned it all. You have several shocks ahead of you.'

He checked what looked like a ludicrously expensive watch. I wondered, briefly, if he had bought it to celebrate our success. 'We're leaving this room shortly,' he said. 'That's going to be your first shock. So, how many of you have been out on the floor yet?'

None of us had. Charlie pulled a little face. His whole mood had changed today. He had never been this animated before. It was almost funny. 'No one ever spoken to you? All the big cats ignored you? Left you all alone in the playground?' he mocked. 'That's how it always is. We've kept you locked away in this nunnery for a reason. We've wanted you to focus. But now you're done, you need to face another reality. We've made room for you on the floor, and you'll start first thing tomorrow. You're ready to trade. It's time to meet the animals.'

# Chapter 10

THE COMPANY'S MAIN TRADING floor was directly above us. It took a matter of seconds to get there in the lift. But it was as if we had been lifted into another world. The noise hit us first. That and the emotion. Straight away you sensed a feeling of competition that bordered on fury.

The place looked to be the size of a football pitch – or possibly ten football pitches. It was entirely open plan, a vast compilation of desks, monitors and yet more monitors. Everyone before us, a sea of young men in shirtsleeves, were coloured by the flickering lights of their screens, then bleached by fierce white ceiling light. Big money could be made here. None was spent on making it anything other than utterly serviceable. The front office is all about efficiency. Nature programmes go on about the harsh environments of Alaska or of the Sahara desert, but they had nothing on this Canary Wharf office.

'What the hell was that?' Martin asked as Charlie led us down between the desks to our stations. A massive smash had reverberated around the office. It sounded like an explosion. But my group of gimps were the only ones who seemed to hear it. No one else looked up from their screens. Charlie had barely registered it. 'That would have been Roach. Sometimes he gets out of control,' he said, when we asked again. It turned out Roach was situated right next to some window blinds. The blinds were full of holes made by his fists. Apparently the company had long since stopped replacing the damaged goods because whenever they did he just punched his way back through the next set. By the look of him, he could have punched through a brick wall. He was standing up and swearing at a colleague by the time we approached. He was probably in his early thirties, taller even than Charlie but nowhere near as polished. He could easily have worked the door at a nightclub. He looked as if he could possibly make a bit of cash at one of the Thursday night white-collar fight clubs the gimp boys were always talking about.

Twenty desks had been cleared for us, scattered throughout the office. Charlie led us around the floor allocating them. We must have looked like kids being dropped off one by one from a day at school. Tobias was first to find his home, in a corner furthest from the door. David was found a desk right in the middle of the room, Lisa was positioned near the door and so on. The roll-call went on, the crocodile of kids trailing behind Charlie got ever shorter until my turn came. I got the desk next to Roach. I tried to read the look in Charlie's eyes as he pointed me towards it. Was this another test of my character? If so, I was up for it. If Charlie thought I'd quit because I didn't like the company I was expected to keep, then he'd have to think again. I'd have sat next to Charles Manson if that's what it took to win.

'I'm Suzana. Nice to meet you.' I reached out my hand to Roach. Then I introduced myself to the other men in my section. The closest one was a fiery-eyed, dark-haired bloke of about thirty. His name was Gordon, and he winked when he said hello. The next two men were further away and they gave distracted greetings as they focused intently on their screens. I had given each of them a firm handshake and looked them right in the eye. I was remembering something Paper-Plane Simon said when he'd met me to talk about trading what felt like a dozen lifetimes ago. 'You want to know why bankers are such cocky bastards when you see them out at night?' he had asked rhetorically, reeking of strange self-satisfaction. 'It's because they've been faking cockiness for so long at work they can't turn it off. So if you ever make it, you'll have to fake it yourself the moment you walk into the office. That's your armour. Traders can smell fear. They go for the kill if they see weakness. So if you ever get on a floor, show them you're their equal.' I'm sure he never imagined that I would ever need that little nugget of advice. But it served me quite well when I met Roach and the gang. If they thought I was some little girl who'd run away at the first sign of trouble, they were about to have a reality check.

'Get familiar with your systems and your surroundings. I want you ready to trade from the moment the market opens tomorrow,' Charlie had said before taking us on to the floor. I looked around me as I sat down. I could see Tobias tapping on his keyboard about a mile away. I might have known he'd be the first to get going. Across the room, David was standing talking to his neighbour, a guy who looked like a slightly older mirror image of himself. I was alone. Roach and the others ignored me. Apart from Lisa in the distance I couldn't see a single other girl anywhere, and for the first time in quite a while I got the old feeling that I was somehow expected to fail. They had me there to fulfil a quota, but they were semi-hoping I would do badly. That way they could say they'd tried but the whole 'female trader' thing hadn't worked out.

I pushed the thought away and got ready to kick off. I had only four monitors on my desk. That picked me out as a beginner, apparently. Roach and all the other senior traders had eight. So what? I'll still make money. I could do it with one monitor if I had to.

I checked my log-in details, got my systems up and running and looked around one more time. On each of our desks we had television monitors attached to pillars that hung from the ceiling at various points. A couple had financial news channels on. But most seemed to be showing sport. How bizarre, I thought, as my eyes flitted from football to rugby to football again.

'Get your phone. Hit the blue button, halfway down on the right-hand side,' Roach shouted at me suddenly. I picked up my phone and found the button he was describing. I had the commentary for the football. 'Hit the black button below it,' he shouted again. Now I could hear the rugby.

'Thank you, that will help me a great deal tomorrow morning,' I shouted back when I hung up. I'd tried to get just enough sassy sarcasm into my voice and my smile. I wanted Roach to know I could dish as well as I could take. His faint smile suggested he might actually have approved. I chalked it down as a tiny victory. I don't know why, but I felt I could learn to like this guy. Don't they say, if you want to be the best then you need to learn from the worst? Roach was never going to be an easy neighbour. But sitting next to him would be, well, educational. It certainly wouldn't be dull.

I heard him rapping his knuckles on the desk again as I focused on my own monitors. I had news feeds, market statistics and all the modelling programmes we had used in the training room. What can I trade? I tried to filter out the noise and the distractions. What was the market rhythm today? This was the feeling I'd been looking for since I'd entered the City. One mouse click from the market and everything it could offer. One day from doing it for real.

I played the markets in my head for about an hour, doing dummy trades and banking virtual profits. In our training room, the boys had sometimes granted me grudging respect for beating the market with unconventional trades. I put it down to my musical training. The thing with music is that it emphasises finding rhythms, patterns, intervals and themes, and I subconsciously applied this training to market data, using chart patterns, technical analysis, doji candlestick patterns and resistance levels. I simply applied Schenkerian analysis to finance.

But Schenkerian analysis is a subjective, not an objective, method. This means that there is no mechanical procedure for arriving at an analysis for a given piece of music; rather, the analysis reflects the musical intuitions of the analyst. Therefore, this analysis is more art than science; a very non-traditional way of analysing the markets. Most people who work in the City are not taught to think this way – they are engineers, mathematicians, physicists etc. Very smart in their own right, but most cannot think laterally, or 'outside the box'. You could also argue that, in part, this narrow-mindedness contributed to the dangers that caused the current financial crisis.

But how would I do out here amidst the traders? Were they sensing the same things about the market? Every now and then, I pulled myself out of my bubble and looked around. I realised that I'd never get any non-verbal trading tips from colleagues. At any moment, the guys nearest to me behaved differently. Roach could be silent and motionless, leaning back with his arms folded, a pair of clean-soled, handmade shoes on his desk. Was he waiting to pounce on some deal? I had no idea. With Roach immobile, Gordon sometimes took over the drama. When I glanced over that time, he was a ball of energy, glancing hysterically from screen to screen. Slightly further away, the other traders could be heard whispering harsh, guttural phrases into their phones, or arguing fiercely, as if the market had just inflicted some personal injustice on them. Every time I looked up, there was a new dramatic episode. In theory, we were all investing in exactly the same markets, with the same instruments, using the same analytical tools. Yet we kept our secrets. In a room of eighty traders, there were eighty different styles of trading.

I wore a cocoon of false confidence when I left home before six the next morning. I wrapped myself deeply in it as I navigated the maze of desks towards the senior traders for my first day of trading. The office was hot and smelt of bacon. People were eating sandwiches with super-sized coffees at their desks, building up energy and preparing for battle with the markets.

'Morning, Roach,' I said. 'Morning, Gordon.'

'We didn't scare you off yesterday, then?' Gordon asked, winking again. Did he always wink when he spoke?

'If you'd worn that shirt yesterday you might have done,' I said. I had a feeling that attack would be the best form of defence with these boys. Something else told me that the more childish the attack, the more effective it would be.

I was right. 'She sounds like your ex-girlfriend, mate,' Roach said, putting his hand out for me to high-five. Gordon shot me with an imaginary gun but clearly approved of the comment. If I could keep that sort of thing up for a year or so, then maybe I'd survive.

I sat down, settled in and logged on. Time to tune out the boys. With round-the-clock markets, we could pretty much make money anywhere and anytime. My basic hours would be seven till five. Ten hours. Ten minutes to go. The former gimps and I had been assigned embarrassingly small trading limits – thank you very much, Mr Reclusive Billionaire. The company mantra was that we could take whatever risks we wanted within our allocated size. If we made money, we split the profits 60-40 with the firm. If we lost money, then the firm would cover it – but we wouldn't survive very long if we continued to performed as such. Having said that, I wasn't planning on making much money my first day. I'd be the tortoise, not the hare.

There were clocks everywhere. On the walls and the ticker tape snaking across the ceiling, and on all our computer screens. It was six-fifty-nine. I tried to ignore the smell of dead meat. I tried to ignore the hot and claustrophobic feel of the office. I tried to ignore the fact that Roach and Gordon were both staring at me as the markets opened. I succeeded. At 7 a.m. exactly, I was ready to trade. Blue and red figures were flashing on my X-trader screens. I was charting patterns on my other monitors. And I was in.

'What the fuck are you doing?! What did you do that for?' It wasn't even 8 a.m. on that first day and Charlie was furious. I'd not seen him so far that morning and I had no idea how long he'd been standing there. I explained my trade to him, well aware that Roach and Gordon were both listening intently. Charlie's face was expressionless. He shrugged and moved away. Was that approval or had he given up on me? I had no idea. So I threw myself back into my screens. If I was doing well, it was only the beginning. If I was messing it up, that was something else altogether.

For the remainder of the day Charlie crept up on me roughly once an hour. He fired questions and demanded instant applications for what I was trading. He did the same for the rest of the first week. 'Look, your boyfriend's back,' Roach would say if he saw Charlie approach me. He and Gordon made kissing noises as Charlie barked orders at me. Charlie gave them the finger as he walked away. After a while, I did the same, whether Charlie was there or not. They seemed to like it.

What I liked was making money. Everything I had imagined about trading was coming true. You really cannot replicate the buzz of being right in the market – it's the greatest rush. Most of my positions were profitable throughout that first week. I had answers for all of Charlie's increasingly hostile questions, because I sensed that I was doing OK. I still wasn't making huge profits – I wasn't trading with much more than one hundred pounds at a time, chump change compared to what would come later. But I'd never intended take huge risks straightaway. I wanted to build my size gradually, learning how the reality of the market differed from the simulation in the training room. It seemed important to know what it felt like when the hedge funds came into the market. I wanted to know what the signs were when some algorithmic trading programme kicked in from the exchange cyberspace.

Futures trading – the kind we were performing – is a zero-sum game. If I made, say, a thousand pounds, it meant that someone, somewhere, had lost it. You never find out who the losers are – the market is too vast and global to know your enemies with such accuracy. But you get an extraordinary sense of triumph when you're the one with profits, or 'in the black'. The boys might have wanted to do more and do it faster. But the boys might be given more leeway if they lost. I had a feeling that Lisa and I wouldn't be treated so kindly. I'd been fired already over a trivial loss and I wasn't about to let that happen again.

My focus became absolute. In the futures market, it has to be. It's not just that things can change over lunch. They can change when you nip out to the loo. When you get distracted. When you blink. Profits can turn to losses when you run to the vending machine for chocolate. I recalled how the hours had dragged in my first two City jobs. Now they flew by. Entire days passed buried beneath a swirl of economic data announcements, market news and numbers on ticker tapes, and constantly changing price data graphs, all set against a *CNBC*-soundtrack.

The banter, insults and jokes with the guys lightened the atmosphere as well. As we got to know each other, they became obsessed with what I wore. They commented on every piece of clothing. So I retaliated. I took the piss out of their other obsessions and idiosyncrasies as well.

There was something tribal about the floor. The guys had football mascots on their desks, and you could wind them up just by looking, laughing and walking away. Their lucky charms were even more fun. Our job may have been exclusively about numbers, but it didn't stop the devotion to rituals, the need to touch a rabbit's foot or coddle a childhood lucky charm before an important economic announcement. Gordon, in particular, was always mumbling not-so silent prayers to God. As far as he was concerned, the market didn't just move, it moved for or against him personally. 'You need professional help,' I'd declare the obvious. I hadn't realised yet that by this stage paranoia was an occupational hazard.

In those first few weeks, I couldn't have felt more at home in our fifteenth-floor madhouse. Nor could I have felt more comfortable with the animals, i.e. the senior traders, and we enjoyed a kind of trading honeymoon period. Making money was still easy in 2006. I had no idea how fast things would change when it turned sour. Or how quickly we would all turn on each other.

# Chapter 11

'**C**OME ON, WE'RE TAKING you out to get wasted.' Roach and Gordon stood next to my desk. I'd had a reasonable day. I'd traded about twenty times and banked around £1,500 in flat markets. And I'd only had four interrogations from Charlie. That must be progress.

'I can't go out with you guys if you're going to dress like that,' I said, looking them up and down. 'I do have a reputation to consider.'

'We know all about your reputation, honey. That's why we want to get you wasted,' said Gordon, winking even more furiously than normal.

I headed out of the office, trying to hide my self-satisfied grin. This was the first time I'd been asked out drinking with the senior traders. Maybe I'd finally been accepted. We headed across a little bridge to a bar I'd never been to. It was literally stuffed with senior traders from our floor. Tobias was there with David, but apart from them, I couldn't see any of the other ex-gimps.

Roach and Gordon practically came to blows over who would put their credit card behind the bar for our little group. At one point I offered to use mine and they nearly killed each other. They'd have died before letting a girl purchase drinks. Then we dived into the crowd. Every sub-group from our floor was represented. There were the Essex boys, keeping up a running commentary on sport, market, girls, market, sex and, yes, the market. They seemed to be doing exactly the same in the bar. Then there were the loud and impossible-to-embarrass Etonians, who took months to figure out that they weren't going to move the market in their favour by calling up one of their aristocratic connections. I also got a closer look at some of the office cokeheads, young guys in their late twenties who appeared to be in their late forties from years of strippers, copious amounts of booze, cigarettes, and late nights followed by 7 a.m. market opening. As one of the most vocal drugged-up traders on the floor (and that's saying something), 'Crazy B', taught me all the French swear words within six weeks of joining. He would often mumble loudly to himself, oscillating between French and English, shouting at the market or to himself, not unlike a mental patient. From a bird's-eye view, our workplace could have passed as a nuthouse.

Money and the markets were the primary topics of conversation in the bar that night. Money, markets and masculinity, to be precise. The language on the floor was never tame, but in the bar it was excruciatingly vulgar. Am I in a bar or a locker room, I thought to myself that first night. If I was the sort to swoon and cry sex discrimination, I could have made a fortune recording things that night. A gay man could have made even more. The discussions went way beyond clichés of big swinging dicks. Every topic the boys dabbled in used crude sexual innuendo. It began with how they wanted to nail some trade or exactly how (and where) they would shaft or screw a fellow trader. It ended with a colleague's incredible over-the-top description of yesteryear. He was an older guy named Stephen I'd never seen, let alone met, before. Roach introduced us and everyone started talking about how much the City had changed. Cue Stephen. 'The City in the eighties was one long hard-on,' he began. 'Everyone had the horn, every thrusting merchant banker, every double-dealing broker, every hard-nosed, limp dick lawyer – they weren't too fussy who they screwed. Clients came, clients went. Here today, screwed tomorrow. And was all this frenzy about reshaping British business? Forget it. It was all about size! Who could pull off the biggest deals? Who could command the biggest fees? Who had the biggest cock in town? That was what it was all about.'

'And that's different to today, how?' Roach asked. None of us had an answer.

We carried on drinking a solid five hours after the market closed. No wonder most of the traders aged so badly. That's what happens when your diet consists of cigarettes, chocolate, booze and both kinds of coke. I lost sight of Roach and Gordon about an hour before I left the bar. Stephen calmed down a bit and actually became quite good company. His less sexually explicit descriptions of the way the City changed were pretty interesting.

He also kept a bit more distance once he'd realised that my wedding ring was real. 'Your husband is a very lucky man,' he slurred.

'Yep, he is,' I concurred. 'But he may not be my husband for much longer if I never get to see him.' I put my drink down, told Stephen I was going to the Ladies and instead headed out towards the cobbles of West India Quay. The skyscrapers' dazzling lights sparkling in the water below were deviously alluring.

Domineering. Brazen. Sexy. Flamboyant adjectives have always described not only high-octane City jobs, but also the general City atmosphere. In a moment of clarity, it struck me how fast this artificial, sterile place had become my home. For the past eight or ten weeks, I hadn't spent time with anyone who didn't work in the City. I couldn't remember when I last thought of anything except my trading limits.

But while the City of London has been raiding and trading since Roman times, Canary Wharf is a modern-day phenomenon. As recently as 1999, just before the opening of the Jubilee line, there were only 15,000 people working amidst those docks, and well over half the office space remained empty. Today its tenants include a laundry list of massive investment houses, including Morgan Stanley, Citigroup, HSBC, Barclays, the bank formerly known as 'Lehman Brothers', the Bank of New York, Credit Suisse, Northern Trust, Bank of America, Bear Stearns (before it was purchased by Square Mile-based firm JP Morgan in March 2008), and the supposed watchdog of all these cowboys, the Financial Services

Authority. But the real significance of the Wharf comes from what it replies. These docks were, just decades ago, the busiest industrial ports in the world. They serviced huge areas of East of London and beyond. We've gone from making real goods to making false bids. Today, instead of balancing smelly fish on their backs, the Wharf workingmen rush around with smelly Reebok sports sacks, and juggle seven flashing monitors with beeping blackberries. And now, of course, there are 'Wharf women'. But not many.

I got a taxi home, kept the window open, and hoped the cold air would sober me up. I wanted to apologise to Alex for being so consumed at work, and for being so late tonight. As it turned out, I didn't get the chance. He was already in bed. It doesn't matter, I told myself as I climbed in next to him. I'm established now. I'm part of the crew, and everything is going to get a lot calmer and a lot easier.

There was nothing calm about the office the next morning. 'Lisa's gone.' The email from Tobias came through at the start of our second hour of trading. 'Her desk has been cleared,' confirmed one of the other gimps shortly afterwards. 'Charlie won't say anything, but watch yourself because he's not a happy bunny,' wrote a third.

We all went for a very quick lunch at roughly the same time that day. That was pretty much a first since we'd gone live. None of us knew what happened with Lisa, and the rumours flew.

'She was so bloody good on the Sim,' David pointed out.

'She struggled with reality,' said Roger, who had been sat closest to her on the main floor. 'Charlie spent more time with her than anyone else. He didn't just fire off a question then walk away. He was there for five, ten minutes at a time and she was only getting worse. He got angry.'

'So she was losing money?' I asked. 'Does anyone know how much or for how long?' Those were the big questions because the answers might one day affect us. How much could we afford to lose to avoid the same fate? We got Tobias to get some gossip from the secretaries, though it was unlikely they'd know any relevant figures. We tried to work out if she'd jumped or been pushed.

'I was in early this morning and I didn't see anyone clear her desk,' said David.

'I'm certain I saw her leave as normal last night so when the hell did it happen?' asked Roger. We talked a bit more, then realised that none of us had her mobile number or a clear idea of where she lived.

It was a wake-up call about how brutal life in the City could become. I'd got a bit carried away with the jokes and the banter. I'd probably become a bit addicted to the constant stream of information. Trading was all-consuming – and I thrived on the daredevil challenge and the potential for glory. I'd forgotten that there was no safety net under us.

We were quiet in the lift as we headed back to the floor. 'Poor Lisa,' I said, to no one in particular as we returned to our desks. The first day I met her I'd wondered whether the City wanted a girl like her or a girl like me. Now I guess I had my answer. Our floor wasn't totally male. But the select few female traders were all immaculately dressed. They made an effort, however stressed-out they became. That's what I did and it's what Lisa refused to do. She'd worn the same shapeless clothes every day and tied her hair back in the same bun. In a job like this – non-client-facing – this shouldn't have mattered. Trading is one of the most non-political, image-irrelevant jobs in the world. It is a business where you should be able to wear a bag over your head and as long as you make money, no one will give a monkeys. That is, unless you're a woman.

The boys got away with absurd fashion choices. Roach and Gordon sometimes wore pyjamas or gym clothes at their desks and they were office heroes. But Lisa got ridiculed for wearing pretty much the same thing and now she was gone.

I traded like a demon that afternoon. Somehow I felt the market's rhythms and my trades ticked up just the way I wanted. By the close, I'd made more in three hours than I'd ever made in a day. But no one noticed or cared. We had all become clinically secretive. We didn't crow about our successes, because we didn't want anyone to notice our failures.

I joined the swarm of humanity heading towards the Canary Wharf Tube escalators at the end of the day. It seemed a long time since I'd felt the wind on my face riding home on Alex's motorbike.

'Shall we go away this weekend? We could get a last-minute deal.' That evening I'd cooked sea bass and tried not to talk too much about Lisa or any of the other people Alex wouldn't know. Instead, we talked about his job and colleagues. It seemed that George, the posh old-timer I'd liked the most when we'd met, had suffered a minor heart attack. He was in hospital in Wiltshire but hoped to be back at his desk within the week.

'Why would he do that?' I asked. 'Doesn't he basically own Wiltshire? He must have more money than he can spend. But he still wants to risk killing himself in the Canary Wharf trading pits just to prove he's got balls? What's that all about?'

'It's not just male pride,' Alex said, sensing where I was going. 'I bet if you were signed off sick you'd be desperate to trade again so they knew you were still in the game. What was the first thing you did when you heard about Lisa? You traded. You didn't go to HR to get her address for a good-luck card. You didn't find her a lawyer. I'm the one person in the City who believes that women are as tough as men, and it's you that proves it.'

I couldn't answer that and I couldn't decide if I'd been insulted or complimented. All I knew was that Alex was probably right. Who on earth would have thought of sending Lisa a good-luck card? Or email? That's when I changed the subject and suggested we go away. After so many years working out the cheapest times of the year to travel, how fantastic to have the cash to hop on a plane whenever we wanted. 'We could go to Corsica or to Monaco. Which do you prefer?'

'I'd love us to but I can't. I need to study this weekend. It's my turn for all that,' Alex said. The constant quest for qualifications was clearly the curse of the two-career City couple. Alex had a new set of professional exams to pass – the FSA. 'Well, let's go on a bike ride out to the countryside on Saturday night,' I said. 'Let's find a country pub and hope the weather's good.'

Alex nodded but didn't seem convinced. He studied for the rest of the night and I watched some crap on TV. What bothered me was the sense that I was wasting time. I'd rather have been trading.

I no longer needed a coffee to wake me up in the mornings. I could walk right past the vast vending machines on the edge of the trading floor. I was addicted to the markets. I got my first morning fix from anticipation. I loved the relative quiet when we all arrived, and the build-up as we waited for the markets to open. Throughout the day I thrived on the peaks and troughs of noise as statistics were released, company news filtered out and good and bad economic news was revealed.

Working alongside Roach, Gordon and the other senior traders pumped up the volume. Until I became a trader, I don't think I'd ever heard a grown man scream. Roach did it all the time. While everyone else kept to himself or herself, he would yell out, both in anger and joy. There were times he resorted to violence, and lashed out at the blinds or anything else within reach. Back in the training room, Charlie had handed us a price list and told us how much would be taken out of our salary for every item we damaged. Crush a mouse and it will cost you £40. Fist through a screen? £400. Break your desk? £4,000. At the time it seemed crazy. But while Roach never pushed his fist through a screen when I was there, he did slam one off the back of his desk when one of his trades went against him.

Naturally, he never got billed for it. The managers closed their eyes to almost every bit of verbal and physical violence as long as you made money in the end. Roach always did. If he'd lost big by lunch, he'd normally make it all back by the close. It was extremely rare for one day's loss to translate into two. I was mesmerised by his drive. I'd learned so much from Charlie but now I was training alongside a very different beast and, once again, I lapped it up. At first, the swearing and smashing seemed like some kind of macho trading floor epidemic. But I found out that it was contagious. I swore and smashed along with the best of them when the markets didn't go my way.

One day the non-farm payroll numbers went utterly against my position, ruining an entire morning's profits, and I genuinely wanted to hurl my monitor across the room. Instead, I got up and strode off to the Ladies. The toilets in anonymous City banks are the most restful places on earth – the one reliable oasis bankers can find when they need to escape the madness. Or a bit of stress sex, as you can find if you wander into them late at night. That day I just stood amidst the rich, white marble and the disinfected surfaces and tried to calm my breathing down. Then I realised that I didn't want to. I'd left my desk because something inside me said I should be ashamed for wanting to destroy my monitor. I looked at my face in the mirror. I wasn't ashamed. I'd felt something out there on the floor. It was anger, frustration, maybe even rage. And it felt, well, great. It made me feel alive. Why should I always be the good girl? Why should I always behave? The boys behaved outrageously every day and were applauded for it. It was time I crossed the line for good and joined them.

I headed back to my desk, energised and ten feet taller. I hadn't been to the gym in weeks but I'd never felt fitter. 'Can't handle the pace, love? Needed a lie-down, did you?' Gordon asked, smirking with sarcasm, as I sat back down. He always made some comment whenever I left my desk, normally something sexist and potentially actionable, but good-natured.

'For once, mate, I can't even be bothered to think of an insult to throw back at you,' I said. 'Not even about your hairline.' Then I got back into the market for the rest of the day. That was where I felt at home.

'If ordinary people get addicted to horse racing they get treatment. If we get addicted to this we get promoted,' Gordon would say. I gave him a high-five for that. Who cared if all our values had been turned on their heads? I no longer cared about life outside of our trading floor. All I wanted to do was click into the world's biggest legal casino and prove I could win.

'Why did you put that trade on? What on earth were you thinking?' It had been ages since Charlie crept up on me and questioned my performance. Strangely, I'd missed him, as had Roach and Gordon, judging by the sound of the orgasms they were faking on the other side of the desks. At least, I hope they were faking them.

I talked Charlie through my most recent decision. A month ago I'd been nervous about his reactions. Now I was interested in his thoughts. All I ever wanted to do was talk about trading, and I was now trading up to fifty times a day. I was exhausted every night, but I'd happily sit in the office for an extra two hours each night reliving what I'd done that day. I just wanted to learn more, keep improving and keep the game rolling. There was an intensity within me that never seemed to fade.

'You're doing OK,' Charlie said as he walked off to someone else's desk. That was the highest praise I could expect to get from him, and indeed, I was remarkably pleased with myself. I scanned the markets for a while and checked my positions were safe. It was nearly 2 p.m. and I was ready to head down to lunch when a message from Charlie hit my inbox. I opened it. It was perfect – he was increasing my limits. It meant that the big boss, via Charlie, was offering me more of his money to gamble every day. Limits are the ultimate status symbols in trading. They can be cut or increased instantaneously – and everyone on the floor was obsessed with keeping their personal limits secret, whilst discovering what everyone else had.

As it turned out, I wasn't the only one to have their limits increased that day. Charlie had been watching us like a hawk, recording our every trade and examining each day's P&L. He'd liked what he saw. With Lisa gone, a solid group of traders remained who might really last the course. That increased our stock all round. We all got more respect from the senior traders as they gradually decided that we might be sticking around. So they decided to let us go out with them. We were invited on a series of wild nights in late 2006, a fantastic boom time for the City – the last of them, as it turned out. But boy, was it good while it lasted. The gimps and I were finally going to taste just how wild the City lifestyle could be.

# Chapter 12

THE BOYS ALWAYS HEADED west when they wanted to drop some serious cash. Nights out on the Wharf were for amateurs, Roach said. They were the dress rehearsals. The West End was where the real action was, and better hunting for girls – not that I cared about that. 'You sure you're up for this? It's guaranteed to be quite obnoxious debauchery,' Gordon had warned in the taxi from Canary Wharf the first time I'd been invited out on one of their regular gambling nights.

'Count me in,' I said.

Our first stop of the night was outside a club just off Regent Street. The security guys on the door seemed to recognise us, or at least they recognised our type. We were waved straight through the velvet ropes. By the time the first of us got downstairs, a sexy Australian girl had cleared a table for us. An equally sexy young waitress was hovering ready to get our first drinks. What I noticed immediately was how well we fit in. I'd imagined that a big group of sleep-deprived men in suits would be terminally uncool in a big West End club. But the guys became cool as soon as they opened their wallets. It's like the line about short rich men who

173

look very tall when they stand on their wallets. If the same principal had applied to us that night, we would have bashed our heads on the ceilings.

'It costs £700 for this table' Roach told me as we settled down. Someone had ordered us a bottle of Grey Goose, which was quickly followed up with a £1,000 bottle of champagne as well. I have no idea what vintage or brand it was. I doubt if Roach or anyone else did either. But those facts didn't matter. The champagne cost £1,000. That alone made it fabulous.

No surprise that our beautiful blond waitress never strayed far from our table. The club was buzzing, but she never made eye contact with any other customers.

'One for the road, then it's time for some real fun,' Roach said after less than an hour in the club.

We left the club just as quickly as we'd raced in. 'See you gentlemen again soon,' the sexy Australian girl drawled as we left. Roach flagged down a couple of cabs to take us on to Mayfair. We were dropped off on a gilded street just past the heavily guarded Saudi embassy, and I watched the boys as they paid the fare.

We were heading for the casino at 50, St James's, a private club I would get to know very well while the good times rolled. In these lush surroundings, you could gamble the old-fashioned way – classy, restrained and financially lethal. That night, my fellow masters of the universe pulled some bad cards. I saw three of them lose a combined total of nearly £20,000. The money disappeared in less than an hour, but the boys didn't seem to care. Losing money merely gave them a chance to demonstrate they could afford it. I also had the peculiar feeling that the more the boys lost, the happier they became. In their twisted minds, this proved just how rich they were. This has got to be the business opportunity of a lifetime, I thought as I watched the cards fall. If I leave the City, I'm setting up the most obscenely expensive casino London has ever seen. I'll rent tables for £1,000 a night and sell £1,000 champagne for £2,000. Taking money off City Boys was a hell of a lot easier than making it alongside them.

'We're right up there with the whales,' Lee said with pride, as he knocked back another obscenely expensive glass of Scotch – it was the nickname the casino gave to their biggest, richest customers.

'I can think of another word that begins with a "w". You're that as well,' I whispered in his ear as we left the tables. The fastest way to earn a City Boy's respect was through an insult.

Anyway, one policeman's salary lighter, we all left the casino room and trooped downstairs to the nightclub. It was packed, even on a Wednesday night. A group of standard-issue Russian models were in one corner and, naturally, my guys wanted to impress. So did they try to break out the Russian phrasebook? Old-fashioned charm? Why bother when cold, hard cash does the trick so effortlessly. They arranged to have ten bottles of Krug sent to our table – with sparklers burning in the top of each. For the boys, it did just the trick – they got the models' attention so I was pushed along our banquette a bit to make room for their slender frames and improbable cleavage. Our ten bottles were drunk in less than two hours. Was I the only one who noticed how little the girls drank and how alert they remained? The guys gradually paired off with one of the girls, one by one, as the night continued. Was it accident or design that there were equal numbers? I sat back and watched their periodic disappearance to the toilets. So this was a normal night out for the City Boys and their 'friends'. I thought of the evenings I'd spent on the river boat with Jason a few years earlier. That was sweet. This was raw.

About three hours later, I would discover how their late-night debaucheries usually ended. We took a trip to a hastily reserved suite in a hotel – tonight, it was the Park Lane Hilton but apparently they had several favourite places for just such an opportunity. By the time we arrived, I was an honorary boy, treated as one of the lads. Yet it was clear I would be an unnecessary puzzle piece after the lights went down so. I made my excuses and dashed out of the hotel lobby.

The boys didn't even notice I'd gone. The next morning at 7 a.m. sharp – only a few hours later – they were all at their desks, as bright-eyed and bushy-tailed as if they'd been tucked in their own beds for a nourishing eight hours. The stamina of the City never failed to amaze me. Just imagine if this vitality were deployed on something genuinely useful. I guess alpha personalities pre-select themselves for their careers. The feeble and the sensitive are weeded out – anyone who can't handle the pace.

\*     \*     \*

The good news was that gambling and chasing women weren't my new pals' only off-duty activities. Their third and fourth favourite hobbies were sitting around spouting absolute rubbish, then insulting each other. Their inappropriate venues of choice for such vital activities were classy places like Boujis, Mahiki and Bungalow 8. I never thought I'd share the same tables as Saudi princes and Russian oligarchs. Or befriend a bunch of guys whose driving force in life was to outspend them.

The unwritten rule of our nights out was that I never spent a penny. The boys paid for everything. It wasn't generosity or good manners. It certainly wasn't chivalry. Instead, it was all about power and status. The man who pays was, well, the man. Some nights the boys literally fought each other to pay the tab. As usual, all I had to do was relax and pretend that I cared.

A typical night would start with someone jeering about how fat one guy was. Or how bald another one had become. Or how his wife/girlfriend was sleeping with the milkman – as if anyone actually has a milkman any more. We'd all have something to say on each subject. It was insult after insult, round and round. With some half-hearted lechery thrown in whenever girls came within range and got the guys out of their homosocial comfort zones. The humour was aggressive and preventative. Lash out at them before they lash out at you. I realised straightaway that I had two choices. I could be the audience or I could join the performers. I climbed up on to that virtual stage. Roach and Gordon were well aware that I could give as good as I got and I enjoyed proving it to all their mates as well.

'We thought you were only interested in make-up or handbags,' one of the boys said to me in a drunken whisper after an expensive night of insults and sporting nonsense at Mahiki.

'Who thought that?'

'We all did. That's why we didn't want you tagging along. But you're all right.'

I smiled all the way home in my taxi that night. 'You're all right' was the most effusive compliment you could get from an unreconstructed City Boy. At the flat, I woke Alex up to tell him about how I'd been accepted. Obviously, he couldn't have cared less. As I struggled to turn my mind off and sleep, I began to wonder if he was right. Why did it matter to me what the boys thought? Was I as happy as I thought?

The doubts stayed with me for weeks. They even managed to take the shine off the firm's Christmas party. Our reclusive billionaire had paid to set up a vast tented city on a cricket pitch near Moorgate. We had a near life-sized ice sculpture of Michelangelo's *David*, which the boys found wildly amusing for obvious reasons. We had vodka fountains, a live twelve-piece band, and the most beautiful bar staff. We ate Michelin-starred lobster canapés, each few mouthfuls probably costing more than a meal for two on the high street. This was a typical front office celebration. Only a year ago, it would have been the biggest night of my year. Two years ago, it would have been impossible for me even to imagine this excess. But as I danced amidst the entertainers and fended off the gorgeous barmen with their colourful trays of drinks, I realised I was frowning. Suddenly, champagne had started to feel just a little bit, well, boring. Looking cynical and jaded seemed to have become compulsory. Feeling dissatisfied was contagious. I saw my colleagues wave away the canapés and ignore the music. Most of us looked not into the eyes of the people working in the cloakroom but straight through them. It was the same arrogance we displayed at work. But it was out of place and horrible here. Roach and the gang were off to some other strip club after the party. For once, I turned them down. I hoped I could sleep myself into a better mood.

January is the worst time to try and get your head together in the City because in most companies, this is bonus season. None of your righteous values stand a chance of surviving the month, as childhood insecurities resurface and new ones are born. It's a time for dreams and disappointments, a high-end, delusional display of greed, envy and fear. And to think I'd been looking forward to it.

Everyone's earnings were always a safe default conversation when we were tired of all the other nonsense. The ex-gimps and I, new to the year-end bonanza, were particularly obsessed. The phrase 'How much do you think Charlie got when he was trading?'

could start several hours of glorious conjecture. We'd already found out a great deal about him. He had a gorgeous wife, three kids, a house in East Sussex, a flat in Shad Thames and three cars, including a classic Bugatti. I guessed his bonuses probably reached a high of £1.5 million and a low of £500,000. Most of the boys at least doubled that. We were all walking encyclopaedias of bond-market performance by this point, so we could run though the most likely 'good and bad' years of his trading career while waiting for the drinks. If he'd done most of his trading before the Dot Com crash, then his cumulative earnings probably rivalled those of a medium-sized electronics business. In retrospect, it was sad that with so much cash in the bank he still wanted to come to Canary Wharf for 7 a.m. each morning – sadder still that none of us questioned it for a second.

City bonuses were supposed to depend on three key criteria: how much money your bank made over the past year, how your specific team performed and, of course, how you performed relative to your peers. But these stipulations were clearly nonsense. In the boom days, there was still something called a 'guaranteed bonus' – the golden ticket. You could collect this by switching banks every two or three years, provided you were performing well and had some client business to bring in. Getting poached to a rival bank, or merely threatening to do so, could earn you much more, much easier, than doing something irrelevant, like working extremely long hours, or relying on the luck of your trading prowess in the market. There's always been this preposterous idea that City players need to earn more each month than teachers do each year because of our extraordinary talent, and the volatile nature of our employment. Realistically, our most exceptional skill is scamming the system for the maximum possible amount of cash. Meanwhile, it is the mercurial nature of City careers that, in effect, pushes our salaries up so high. We made it a volatile profession by jumping ship as often as we could. That was far easier than doing our jobs well, and waiting to be promoted. All this would only really end when the markets imploded and the music stopped. But in early 2007, we drowned out the warnings that that was ever likely to happen.

So how much would us gimps get? The amount of money we wanted clearly bore no resemblance to the amount of money we needed. Even if, in our late twenty-something, early thirty-something world, someone could justify 'needing' an extra £100,000 a year to help pay for a flash pad, car or social lives, then this wasn't necessarily the figure we aimed for. If your colleagues got a £100,000 bonus then you wanted £150,000. If they got £150,000 – or said that they were – then you wanted a whole lot more on top of that as well.

This abracadabra alchemy had already started to filter into the deals we did on the trading floor. In the office, our P&Ls had become symbols of our virility. But I didn't just want the markets to go my way because I'd make £10,000 before lunch. I wanted them to go my way because that would prove I knew more than you, better than you, sooner than you. That was what we had been led to believe. That was how the banks made sure we kept on raising the bar and making bigger trades. Someone had a theory that the best brokers and traders were people who had been abandoned by their parents or bullied in school. Those people had someone they wanted to get back at – a bone to pick. I don't think I fitted into that category. I'd always loved school and I'd had a brilliant childhood. But I did have people I wanted to get back at: all the people who'd suggested I couldn't make it as a trader or should pick a more 'female-friendly' profession. I wanted to show that they had been wrong about me, as had all the people who said that you could never move up the ranks in the City and that workers who began in the back office would stay in the back office. I might never see any of those people again. They'll probably never know I'd proved them wrong. But at least I knew I'd done it. I was in the front office and I was learning more every day. Bonus time was particularly insightful. There is truth in the idea that the louder, the more obnoxious and the more insecure a trader is the more he or she can make. In our first year, the gimps and I could see that in one brief personal meeting about the bonus pool our colleagues could chase away their demons. Making money gave them self-respect. If they were lucky it seemed their euphoria could last up to an hour before they realised they had to prove themselves all over again for the next year. If they were unlucky then one glance from a smug-looking colleague who may or may not have been paid more could conjure up more insecurity than ever. The whole things was childish and crazy. But it was so much fun to sit ringside at this particular circus.

Big bonus or not, Tobias bought his first flat that spring. He looked at warehouse conversions in Wapping and Georgian mansion blocks in South Kensington, but ultimately settled on a brand-new apartment in – surprisingly – Canary Wharf. His commute was less than ten minutes by foot. 'Can you see the office from your bed?' I asked. Proud, yet sheepishly, he admitted that he could.


Roach and Gordon had new surprises in store for me on our next night out. For some reason they had temporarily given up on the plush sofas, brocade cushions and members-only ethos of the Mayfair clubs. Instead the boys wanted to do some serious vertical drinking in the vast, football pitch-sized bars around Liverpool Street Station. If ever there was a invention hostile to females, it's the no-chairs drinking den. Even in my highest heels, I struggled to be on the same level as the circular counters, let alone my colleagues. Forget about the first female president of the United States. The first woman to get served at The Hamilton Hall will be the one who really makes history. I'm certainly glad my free-spending colleagues meant I didn't ever need to try.

Fortunately we didn't spend too long in those bars. The whole point of them is to get the punters drinking as much as possible, as fast as possible. The boys always obliged. Then we moved on. Brick Lane was normally next on the night's agenda. It was probably no more than ten minutes walk away, but we always went by taxi, which took about twenty minutes if traffic was bad. We'd commandeer a big table in an Indian restaurant, get the curries in, and then start talking nonsense. I kept tagging along on those nights because for some reason the nonsense had started to get a bit more intriguing. One of the global fund managers from the floor above us had begun to come along. He was in his forties, his name was Ollie and he was first Etonian I'd ever met who genuinely made me laugh. Instead of lashing out at others, he charmingly bragged about his bad behaviour. His stories tended to take for ever. He told them loud enough for everyone else in our restaurant to hear too.

'I got so drunk at lunch before an analysts' meeting at an American bank on Gresham Street that the bastards wouldn't let me past Security,' he boomed at an East London restaurant one night. 'The guards physically pushed me out of the lobby and on to the pavement. It was only when I rang the organiser on my mobile that they realised I wasn't some schizophrenic homeless person and let me in.'

'So you went to the meeting?'

'Of course I went to the bloody meeting. I got in there, grabbed the little PR bird by the hand and whispered that I needed a quick glass of white wine to calm my nerves. Somehow her little boss lady at the other end of the room heard about it and put the kibosh on the plan. The little bird only went and got me a cup of coffee.'

'Poor you,' I said, loving it.

'Well, as it turned out, they were holding the briefing in a meeting room with a vast table. I got the milk in the cup without incident. Then I decided I'd have a bit of sugar.' He looked up, not a hair or a shirt cuff out of place and the epitome of Home Counties respectability. 'Now, I don't normally take sugar, so I can't tell you where that thought came from. It may well have been that I was feeling unwell. The analyst, a nervous Yank with preposterous brown hair who looked about nine years old, was spouting off about commodities, or population growth, or greenhouse gases or one of those dreadful things they get so worked up about. I had the spoon halfway to the cup. It was that rather nice sugar, the brown crystals that you can suck. I decided to interrupt the little man and blow me if I didn't drop the spoon. Sugar went everywhere. But I'll say this for Americans. Polite as hell. They carried on regardless. No one said a word about the mess. Nor did they when I decided I would pick up each crystal, one by one, and put the back in the bowl. I had quite a bit of fun doing that, as it turned out. Took longer than I'd thought, perhaps, because even the little boy with the nervous tic had stopped talking by the time I was done. But all in all, a marvellous afternoon's entertainment.'

'Did you ever get invited back?'

'I may have done. I can't quite recall who they were, so I can't be entirely certain. Now, did I mention the time one of the French banks decided to suck up to me?'

Even if he had, it was clear Ollie would tell us again.

The tales went on as those long-suffering Brick Lane guys brought our food. One of Ollie's colleagues, an equally ill-behaved and equally posh analyst called Justin had the best story. It also involved a little too much lunchtime drinking.

'I'd been taken out to La Gavroche by the chief executive and finance director of some dreary little manufacturing company I was invested in,' he began, his voice booming around the room. 'I'd had a few beforehand, the way you do, and I wasn't really focusing on the clients. I excused myself and headed to the Gents to splash some water on my face and wake myself up. Back at the table I took the bull by the horns. "What's the story with the anti-trust legislation in the States? How's that going to affect your exports then?" I asked. Damn me if they didn't have much of an answer. "Do I take it that you won't match last year's targets?" I asked, pretty certain I'd hit a nerve. I'd already decided I'd short the whole stock as soon as I got back to my desk.'

'Have you guessed where this one ends?' Ollie asked me, a huge smile on his face. I had a horrible feeling that I had.

'I was only at the wrong bloody table,' Justin boomed.

'All us men in suits all look alike as you know. Turned out that these people ran an office cleaning company. They must have been doing all right, having lunch in a place like La Gavroche. I should have invested in them, now I think of it.'

'So did you get back to your real hosts?' I asked.

Justin frowned. 'I'm sure I must have done, but I don't actually recall. I think I did sell the company's stock, though. All got a bit too messy, I felt.'

I wondered what effect that drunken lunch might have had on his fund's performance as I got some fresh air in the street after our meal. Clearly none of the others cared. They were all inside, arguing over the bill. That was one of the power things I'd spotted early on. They always argued over the bill when it was brought by a man. If the Brick Lane boys had employed a blonde Russian girl simply to hand over the cheque then they'd have had a lot less stress and earned about four times as big a tip.

'So, where now, guys? A dodgy East End strip club?' I have absolutely no idea why I said those words. To this day, I still can't quite believe they came from my own lips. If I try and understand it, I come up with two theories. The first was that strip clubs were the elephant in the room on all our group nights out – I was convinced that's where they'd go if I were absent. So why should it be any different if I was? If I tagged along, I could finally go about breaking this last taboo.

Or perhaps I said it out of some deep-seated curiosity.

The boys did talk about them all the time. I already felt I knew the difference between the established clubs full of English girls, and the slicker West End ones, full of Eastern Europeans. I'd heard plenty of conversations about how the clubs and the girls had changed since the Eastern Europeans had arrived. It was just after ten on a cold February night and I'd drunk enough to be feeling relaxed, but not too much so as to cause any trouble. Let's slay this demon, I thought. Take me to meet some of your precious girls!

'My dear, I do feel I may have fallen in love with you,' Ollie boomed at me as the lads shuffled their feet. He offered me his arm, the consummate English gentleman. 'If you will walk this way, I can lead you to just such an establishment.'

As it turned out, Ollie only led me as far as Whitechapel High Street where we flagged down a couple of cabs for the remainder of the journey. 'I hope you will do me the honour of taking care of your coat,' he said when we had edged through a very ordinary-looking door in a street about fifteen minutes away. I saw more notes than I had expected change hands at the desk. For some reason I'd thought it would only be a fiver or so to get in. The boys looked to have handed over a couple of twenties each. This had better be good.

'I'm not staying more than ten minutes. I just want to grab a peek, then I'll leave you to it,' I said as we headed downstairs. That's where I got my first surprise. The place was actually pretty slick. It was very modern and trendy, with a dazzling metallic bar. Little groups of men in suits were standing in clusters, being chatted up by the girls – all of whom looked fabulous, to be honest. We got to the bar and the boys ordered some top-quality spirits. They came in huge measures and what looked like five twenties were passed over to pay for them. There were six of us.

We were surrounded by the time I'd taken a sip. The girls looked just as good up close. I'm ashamed to say I'd expected druggie, pock-marked skin. Instead there was just healthy-looking, toned skin – and a lot of it. The girls who'd targeted our gang were in tiny hot pants and crop tops. They were amusingly flirtatious. I swear I really did hear one of them whisper, 'You're a big boy,' at Roach. More hilarious still, he seemed to buy it.

'Fancy a dance?' the girls were all saying. So we headed down another level. The boys had clearly been here before. We were hit by a wall of noise in the lower bar, the music was mind-numbing. This was clearly where the real action took place. I looked around. I took in the stage, the three twenty-foot poles, the curtained-off areas around the edge of the room that I didn't want to think too much about. Three dancers were doing their stuff on stage. They soon made the girls upstairs look fully clothed. There were no secrets when they bent over which, of course, they did constantly. But it was clear that the no-touching rule was very strictly enforced. The girls were in total control. If a man stepped even an inch out of line then he was out of the club. If they didn't like him, or thought he was behaving badly, then he was out on his ear. It was their decision and they made it happen. I liked that.

We were found a set of leather sofas, all very dark, masculine colours. All the other guys seemed to be hideously drunk. My guys, by comparison, were really quite respectable. I felt a sudden and very strange burst of near-maternal pride. I sat through about three cast changes on the stage and several up-close dances at our sofas. This is the moment the guys start to go through to the curtains, I thought. So this is probably my moment to leave. I've been there, seen it and, metaphorically speaking, I've worn the wet T-shirt.

'Thank you for a most marvellous evening,' I shouted at Ollie, all mock gentility. He kissed my hand. I nodded at the other guys. 'I can find my own way out,' I yelled. I really didn't want any of them to stand up at that precise moment.

'First time, love?' the lady said as she found me my coat. 'Are they colleagues of yours?'

'Yes it was, and yes they are,' I said. 'Dare I ask if they are regulars?'

She put a glamorous red-nailed finger to her lips. 'A lady never tells, my dear.'


I stopped socialising for a while after that. I felt I'd seen it all – quite literally in the case of some of the dancers. Alex and I had decided to cut down on the clubbing and joined a new gym in Canary Wharf, a health club so full of fit bodies it resembled a night club. He was increasingly distracted at work but we were still trying to go every second evening. It had an incredible pool, and a panoramic view that gave the sensation that you were an organic part of the steel and concrete architecture growing from the Thames. We were also trying to fend off exhaustion by eating healthily. I was cooking more often and we'd given up rich City restaurants in favour of sleek little sushi bars in Soho and beyond.

'Do you know, I have absolutely no female friends in the City? None at all,' I told Alex one night. 'Sometimes I think there would be more female company on an oil rig.'

'What about Amanda?' Alex asked. The journalist friend I'd met in my early City days.

'She scares me,' I admitted. 'Anyway, all she talks about is men, which sort of defeats the purpose. Once in a blue moon, I'd like to talk about clothes.'

'We could go out for dinner with Ben and his wife again. Or I need to somehow get you into the social side of my office. We're nowhere near as polarised as yours.'

We ended up doing both those things. Ben and his wife Katrina, who was a City lawyer, were a breath of fresh air. I also enjoyed turning up at a few of the leaving drinks and other nights out with Alex's colleagues. But, as usual, I wanted to win the real battle on my own. My firm wasn't entirely male. There were several women among the senior traders and elsewhere in the office. They were the sleek, well-groomed ones I'd always wanted to emulate. We danced around each other for a long time. At first there was the same reticence that kept every gimp alienated from the old-timers, the decision not to waste time with people who might not last the course. Now that I felt I had proved myself over six tough months, I set out to get to know them.

The girl I admired the most was named Stella. She wore the best suits in the office, had the best shoes, the best handbags, you name it. I noticed something else when I occasionally walked past her desk. She had total respect from the men in her team. You could sense it. She hadn't compromised her femininity, she just made money and did her job well. I mentioned her name to a few of the guys sometimes and it seemed that it wasn't just her own team who respected her. She also had a reputation for being one of the brightest traders on the whole floor. She was wicked smart, fast, instinctive and successful.

I occasionally took my eyes off my monitors for the next few days and tried to see when she left her desk for lunch. It wasn't easy to see through the forest of monitors and I had a few false starts when I saw her leave and realised, too late, she was only going to the loo. I didn't think that was quite the right place for an ambush.

On the fourth day of my quest I finally got the timing right. 'Do you mind if I join you?' I asked as I hovered with my tray in the canteen.

'Be my guest,' she said. Not a hint of annoyance or suspicion. Why on earth had I put this off for so long?

'I'm Suzana,' I said. 'I'll be totally honest. I feel I've overdone the testosterone thing lately and I've realised

I don't know anyone apart from the boys on my team. I wanted to spread my wings a bit.'

Stella was delightful. 'It's never a good thing to overdo the testosterone,' she said. Then she complimented me on my jacket. We talked clothes for a good ten minutes.

Instead of prop trading, Stella did a lot of corporate entertaining. It's called 'rainmaking', trying to win new clients and business for her division of our company. That was the crazy, binge-drinking part of the city that the media was so obsessed with. I liked the idea of seeing how a woman handled it. Stella was happy to oblige. 'I'm taking some clients out to dinner next Tuesday,' she said. 'I'm sure we'd love you to join us.'

I was on cloud nine for the next four days. I emailed Stella a couple of times to check what she was going to be wearing.

When the big night came, she wore a fabulously tight black dress while I had thrown my usual office dress code to the wind and worn a multicoloured kimono-dress and my highest heels. We had a reservation at a restaurant a few streets around the corner from the Ritz. For the meet and greet, the pre-dinner drinks and the first half of the meal, I watched Stella and was nearly open-mouthed in envy. She was the supreme hostess. We were entertaining one other City woman and three City men. One of them, in particular, had the power to bring us a lot of extra business and throughout the long meal Stella seemed to be twisting him around her newly manicured little finger. Forget Roach and Gordon and vertical drinking in the Viagra triangle, this is where I want to be I decided. This is the City I want to be part of, I thought as our coffees arrived.

As the bill arrived, it was placed in the middle of the table with admirable political correctness. Stella leaned forward to collect it – and I got my reality check. There was a hand on her knee. Well, a little higher than her knee, to be honest. I flashed a look at her client. He was smiling.

'Let me get everyone some taxis,' Stella said, still in total control as we decanted into the spring air. She looked like a fashion model, flagging cabs down from the kerb. The female client got the first of them, two of the men shared the second. The third was for me. 'See you in the office tomorrow, darling,' Stella said. I'm embarrassed to say I was almost choking up. How silly. How childish. How weak. It was none of my business, but I couldn't look back to see if she got a final cab for her client and if she shared it. When I got home I woke Alex up, banging around the flat in anger.

'How was your girly night out?' he asked. 'Not good?'

'I'll tell you tomorrow,' I said. I made myself a cup of tea before going to bed. I knew it was crazy to feel let down by that evening. I knew that normal rules don't apply in the City. Regulators, ethics committees, things your mother taught you. We earn our big money because we forget about all of that. We all did whatever it took to make money for our company, our team, ourselves. Stella made money. No questions asked.

\* \* \*

I traded in silence the following day. Charlie always said we had to leave our emotions in the lobby, and I never struggled with that. The more clinical I was, the more money I made. I was clinical as hell for the rest of the week.

'What have you done today? Talk me through your trades.' I felt strangely reassured whenever Charlie crept back up on me, as he did that Friday. His presence reminded me that at least one part of the City was constant. He had relaxed a lot since the end of last year. I don't think he was still directly responsible for us any more. He had to keep an eye on us, but his reputation was no longer on the line, and I think he only really checked up on us because he was genuinely interested in our market view. At this point, there was certainly a lot to talk about. At the beginning of 2007, it began to feel like the market was getting tougher and more confusing by the day. Not every trade will go the way you want it to, naturally – how could it? But until this stage, I had always won far more than I lost. Now, I was merely breaking even. The fact that Roach and Gordon had stopped their silly love-ins when Charlie stopped by was another sign of how serious things had become. In early 2007 they wanted to hear his trading ideas as well. That was quite worrying, when I thought about it. So what was going on?

'Things are getting tighter,' Charlie said. 'There are a lot of undercurrents in the market. Trends are going to get harder to call from now on. We'll get through it, but we need to focus.' Roach and Gordon were silent as Charlie walked away. None of us traded for quite some time. Someone, somewhere, clicked half the office TV screens from football to cricket. I hated that bloody game. I looked up and absorbed the spectacle that we managed to call an 'office'. Everyone was there as usual. Everyone was working as normal. But deep down it all felt anything but. My sense of the music in the market had sometimes edged me ahead of the guys. Lately things had started to feel dangerously off key. Warning bells were sometimes ringing in my mind. The credit crunch had begun.

# Chapter 13

**I**'D HAD A BIT of a hunch back in February 2007, when the Dow Jones Industrial Average hit a high of fourteen thousand. My whole body tensed up. I just didn't think it could be right, as there seemed no reason on earth for shares to be that high. Something had to be wrong. Every time I spoke to my family back in the rural Midwest, they had bad news – redundancies, home repossessions, people and businesses going bankrupt by the day. It seemed so different to the America I had left behind. Just before I arrived in London, there was optimism, easy credit, and a buoyant job market for those straight out of university. I'd seen how easy it was for some of my friends to pay for the American dream, even if they were clean out of cash. The sheer amount of junk mail at my parents' home demonstrated just how desperate the banks were to offer as many credit cards to as many people as possible. By 2007, the credit free-for-all was just as deeply established in Britain. There had been a speculative orgy proliferating for years.

I was certain it couldn't last. I thought about the mood of the market all the time. I didn't want to follow the crowd and invest as if the game hadn't changed because I thought it had. One of Alex's friends confirmed it. 'They call it a bottomless pool of credit, but there's no such thing,' he said one night at dinner. 'Every pool has a floor somewhere. When we hit it face-first it's going to hurt like hell.' That man could have won 'pessimist of the year' every year I knew him. He worked in Alex's middle office and was always saying that if he were investing, he'd take every penny out of shares fast.

'That's easy for you to say. You don't have any money in the markets to start with,' Alex would joke.

The trouble was – we did. And it was starting to worry me.

We'd had remote Bloomberg terminal access in our flat from the time we moved in together. I think Alex had always had it. I loved it at first. In the honeymoon period of gimp life, I'd survived on a diet of financial news feeds. I was desperate to learn and was consequently obsessed with data and market trends. Not everyone would want to see the same screens they had at the office get switched on in their living room at night. But I did, at least for a while. It made me feel more connected to the City. It was also an easy way for Alex and I to bond – which was crucial as the markets intensified, and we saw less and less of each other. When other couples might be chatting about holiday plans or the latest films, we talked about the market. Who knew pillow talk about options theory could get so saucy? I remembered Alex's theories and all the experience he had obtained in his extra five years in the City. He passed it on freely, which was refreshing after dealing with the secrecy and psychotic competitiveness of the gimps. In our training room, you were only told things on a 'need to know' basis. At home, I could ask any question. No one would stab me in the back, or make me feel small.

Those domestic conversations made me a better trader. Having unlimited, real-time access to market information at home as well as at work taught me the rhythm of finance far more rapidly. Unfortunately, like most City bankers, we didn't just watch the markets out of hours. We traded on them as well. Very early on, I was introduced to the surreptitious world of personal accounts – or PAs, as they're known.

Whenever we joined them for dinner, Alex's friends Ben and Katrina were constantly bragging about how fantastic their PA was doing. They hinted about a villa on the Riviera in the South of France. They talked about the high-risk strategy they took to earn the highest of returns. It was intoxicating, but precarious. And in 2007 it all went wrong.

'Can you come round?' Katrina called early one evening when I'd just got back from the office. I agreed, slightly bemused. She and Ben were still more Alex's friends than mine but he was at a work do that night and couldn't join us. When I arrived at their flat in Notting Hill, Katrina was on her own and in tears.

'We've lost everything,' she said. One of the bets Ben had taken with their fabled PA had gone spectacularly wrong. The £30,000 stake money he had invested from his 2005 bonus was invested in the highest risk options. In the low volatility period of 2005–2006, this strategy paid off spectacularly. Within only a year, he had turned £30,000 into a £500,000 nest-egg. Fast forward six months, and he clearly ignored the warnings of trouble in the US. He bet the nest egg on the dollar/euro exchange rate deteriorating. But last night, it soared.

'How much did he lose?' I asked as Katrina opened what looked to be an inappropriately expensive bottle of wine.

'About ninety per cent of what we had.'

I'm a maths geek, so I didn't even need to do a sum in my head. 'That still leaves you with more than you started with,' I offered. To City Boys – and City Couples – that didn't matter. The shock of losing took away every ounce of perspective. 'How is he?' I asked. Where is he? I was thinking.

'He's bad. I don't know what to say to him. We could have paid off our flat in Antibes with that money.'

I thought back to the few times our team had lost big in trading. Charlie had always handled it well. He had never gone in for blame or pointless post-mortems. He simply did the constructive criticism thing, and focused on the next time. 'Tell Ben that the world is changing and he shouldn't take so much risk any more. Maybe he should also look longer term.'

I spoke to Katrina again that weekend. She took the phone outside, out of Ben's earshot. She sounded good. 'He's changed,' she said. 'He told me he's going to take less risk.' Of course we all know now that City Boys never really change. Nor do they really get the concept of risk. Over the next twelve terrible months, Ben would apparently make back a huge percentage of his electronic losses. Along the way, however, his trading confidence would be replaced by its ugly sister – unfettered greed. Ben felt so overconfident in his abilities that he encouraged Katrina's parents to give him some of their savings to invest, and also took personal money from a colleague at his bank. That all made him see himself as the 'star trader' again – the one every City Boy aspires to be. But the story played out just the way stock market history suggested it would. Exactly a year after his first trading blow-out, the Chinese announced that they were diversifying out of the dollar. The news had a dramatic effect on the same dollar/euro exchange rate that Ben had been gambling on the previous year. The storm hit him overnight and he had no time to hedge. This time, he lost more than ninety per cent of his money – he lost one hundred per cent. So did Katrina's parents. They were the lucky ones. It turned out that his work colleague had taken out a loan to provide his seed capital. So, as a result, he was now £100k in debt.

When I heard the details, I realised that Ben had done the exact same wrong trade, in the exact same wrong circumstances. It's easy to see why. Go up to a five-year-old boy and ask: What is the next number in the following sequence – 5, 6, 7, 8, 9? He's going to say 'ten'. Ask him again once he's grown up into a City Boy. 'Well, ten seems to be the number that everyone else is going to expect. It's the number people probably picked before. It's a powerful psychological level. So I'll say 8.' It goes back to my old theory that men focus more on being right than they do learning the truth. By entering into the exact same trade, Ben desperately tried to rewrite history. He wanted to prove he'd been right the first time. I swear guys will make the same mistake again and again just so that, by the law of averages, one day they can say, 'I won.' The cost of this egotistical obsession is extremely high. The pressure those losses put Ben and Katrina's relationship under was impossible to miss. Their marriage didn't survive. Two more brittle, strained individuals I don't think I'll ever see. Unless, perhaps, I looked in the mirror.

Fortunately, Alex and I had never gone crazy and we'd never done anything terribly risky with our money. We'd not done the whole insider trading thing on our City nights – though we heard a good deal about it from others. The business conversations 'accidentally' overheard at home. The minor abuses, the way some people buy huge numbers of share in a company just before their other half confirms a merger or acquisition they had discussed the night before.

Our investments were much more sedate. Just as well, because I was learning that money and marriage aren't the best mix. The harder the markets got, the tougher it was to make joint decisions. One of us had to win arguments to make the call. Our funny little pillow talk about options pricing turned ugly. It became a battle. Which of us knew more? Which of us was right? Which of us could prove our point first?

\* \* \*

Back in April 2007, much bigger battles were being fought in Canary Wharf. The snippets of news I received months earlier from America were climbing to the top of British business pages. A large American investment bank that was heavily exposed to sub-prime mortgage lending went bust. Afterwards, we struggled to distinguish which of the thousands of City players was exposed to them. I'd head back to my desk after the morning meeting, when we'd hear the latest market news and forecasts. As I waited for the clock on my screen to tick 7 a.m., there was a noticeable heaviness in my heart.

The pace exaggerated as the market deteriorated, but for extended periods of time, the floor was actually a lot quieter. The banter from Roach and Gordon dried up the moment things got tough. All that shouting and smashing had been showboating for the good times. Intensity was the order of the day for the bad. The guys were now too worried about losing their jobs to make animal noises, or catcalls. My favourite line from Michael Lewis's book *Liar's Poker* had described trading floors as 'a minefield of large men on short fuses waiting to explode'. In London in the late spring of 2007, fuses were as short as hell, but the explosions were postponed. An ominous mood permeated the City and Canary Wharf, as if something terrible was lurking just around the corner. The worst bit was not knowing when that something would occur.

The gimps began taking some real hits. One bright May morning in 2007, we arrived in the office to find that David had quit. In January he had joined the gym in a desperate bid to get his body back in shape. I doubt he had actually put on much extra weight since joining the bank. It was just that the body mass of his muscles had all shifted to his waist. In little more than six months, a fit, broad-shouldered, muscular young man had become just another fat City Boy. I'd seen him on the machines at the gym most evenings almost every day for a month. Others told me he'd been getting up at five every morning to do another work-out before the working day began. He was a classic overly aggressive alpha male, giving a thousand per cent of himself to every single activity. He'd left because of stress, we were told. And at that point, we didn't really know the meaning of the word.

Bravado got us through those difficult days, as well as the City credo that we always know better than everyone else. Trading floors are, to a large extent, popularity contests. Getting popular, thus, maximising your bonus, was easy if you told the bosses what they wanted to hear. In 2007 they wanted to know that the slump was temporary, that volatility would ease, that sub-prime meant nothing and that the UK was safe. The pessimists were ostracised. Risk managers who actually did their jobs were worse than nagging old women to top-performing proprietary traders. No one in *any* front office ever wants to hear about risk. The people who bothered about it worked in the back and middle offices – and as far as traders were concerned those people barely existed. I'd found out the hard way that traders mocked and derided what they saw as the 'little people' further down the greasy pole. Few traders would recognise more than a tiny number of middle or back office colleagues. Many wouldn't even be able to find the office locations on a map. They didn't get the fact that their colleagues examined all the figures, balanced out the trades and often saw the bigger picture. Woe betide the back office boys if they tried to get this message across, though. I heard stories of internal meetings at all sorts of trading firms where front office people laughed at and bullied risk managers who attempted to wave a few red flags about over-the-counter (OTC) derivatives, or counter-party exposure. Traders insisted that everything would be OK, that this time would be different, that no crisis would last for ever. Of course, all these traders ever really thought of was themselves – all they wanted was one more year, one more bonus and *to hell with the consequences.*

'Never bring domestic problems into this office.' That had been Charlie's stark warning. But as the markets deteriorated, mine invariably did intrude. Suddenly, Alex began ringing me during the working day. Never mind that it was the one thing I had never been allowed to do to him. 'What's your P&L like today?' 'Are you up or down?' 'Did you jump on those non-farm figures?' The questions came thick and fast. It was a nightmare. It was bad enough to have Charlie and the other risk managers judge my performance each day. It was unbearable to have Alex do it as well. I began to have serious doubts – perhaps two traders per couple is one ego too many. When I got home, exhausted and looking for a sympathetic ear to vent my crazy day, it drove Alex mad. He could only tell me that his had been crazier. If I made £5k, he'd made £50k. If I lost huge, he had an even worse time – so it was up to me to make dinner. I've gained perspective looking back on those times and thinking how awful life was at home during the credit crunch. At the time, those battles took energy I simply didn't have.

I can't blame what happened next on anything or anyone in particular. But the more exhausted I became, the more likely I was to make a mistake. My moment of truth (or rather, weakness) came in June 2007. It was a brutally hot day by London standards, but all everyone could talk about were icebergs. Just how much toxic debt was out there under the market waters? Could it sink a hedge fund? A bank? The United States?

'This market is going to sort the men from the boys,' we were told at our morning meeting. By then I was so stressed and institutionalised that I didn't consider mentioning the girls. Stella didn't either. She was at the meeting, looking well groomed and dazzling as ever. She hid stress particularly well – not a talent I possessed. Back at my desk, I wanted to get a grip on the volatility. I knew that it was impossible to tame any market. I should have taken that as my cue to be smart, to think strategically, to consider the longer term and to look back to the past. But for that one brief, awful period I took the easy option and found myself wrapped up in the macho herd mentality of the office. Just like everyone else I thought I should trade my way out of trouble, not consider what had caused the trouble in the first place. I forgot about the serious, analytical work that was being done in the back and middle offices. I just focused on the casino-style madness high up in our Canary Wharf tower. The feeling there was that one big bet could always turn everything around. A roll of the dice could consign the credit crunch to history. Carried along by this crazy belief I joined everyone else and started buying boxes of jelly beans from the vending machines before trading began each morning. The sugar made me forget I took almost no breaks.

One day in particular summed up the volatile nature of the market. My first big trade of the day went against me. I cursed it, but in typical trader fashion, I doubled up. I'd get it right the second time. Click. It has to be the bottom now. I have to be right. As the markets ticked lower, it appeared I was wrong.

The market kept going against me. As the hours passed, I lost more and more. It was getting harder to breathe. I'd never struggled like this. I doubled up again. The markets defied me, and I couldn't stop losing.

At my lowest point, I looked up. It was a sub-conscious, guilty check to see if Charlie was nearby. I felt that I could cope with this mess as long as he never knew. I gave another silent prayer. Please, Alex, don't pick this one terrible moment to call.

I turned back to my monitors. The sound of shouting around me indicated that I wasn't alone in having a bad day. But I doubted anyone else was in as deep as me – or falling as fast. In the end, I lost more in the next two hours than I had made in the entire month. It was a shocking amount: £500,000 before lunch. Just before 1 p.m., I freaked out. I didn't swear. I didn't say a word. I kept my eyes down as I walked across the floor to the toilets. *No one notice that my body is shaking. Please can no one see me or speak to me. You're nearly there.* When I was in my sanctuary, the shaking got worse. It was as if some force had taken control of my body. I was alone, breathing hard, forcing my face down on to the marble surface, praying that no one saw me. Not Stella, not one of the secretaries. Please give me this one moment alone to pretend it's not real.

I don't know how long it took me to look in the mirror. This was real. And the day wasn't over. I knew the longer I stayed in that room, the harder it would be to leave.

I took another breath and got it together. I stood up straight again. This was intraday trading. I'd signed up for bad days as well as good. You can lose so much, so fast. But if you're good, you can make it all back.

Roach and Gordon had noticed how long I'd been away.

'You OK?' Charlie was at my side. He had clearly seen my P&L.

'I'm fine. You?' Fake that confidence. 'It's just another afternoon,' I said, logging back on. My awful P&L was still there. But it didn't scare me the way I thought it would. I'd turned it around before. I could do it again.

I traded like a maniac. I fought for every pound I'd lost. In the blur of my losses, I sometimes sensed the boys watching me. I could feel Charlie behind me. I never looked up once. All I saw were my screens and the clock. Three hours to go. Two hours. One hour. The final moments. Then it was over.

In the end, I couldn't make back the full £500,000. But I did make nearly £450,000 that awful afternoon. I ended the day down £50,000 – a headteacher's salary. It's a good amount of cash. But it wouldn't destroy me.

'We're going for a drink,' Charlie said. I sat on one of our usual banquettes in one of our bars, barely able to see straight, or focus. But I remember what he said. 'This job is no longer about how you are when you're up. It's how you are when you're down. You did OK.' Then, as always, he moved the conversation on past P&Ls. He talked about what I could learn next time.

Alex wasn't there when I got home that night. I didn't remember him saying anything about a meeting or night out, but with the markets in such a chaotic state, I didn't expect to always know where he was. A huge part of me was actually glad. I needed to be alone that evening. I had to let my mind leave that day behind. I also realised I had to eat. I'd got through that day on nothing but coffee and two packets of jelly beans.

Without adrenaline, I had nothing left to give. And our kitchen was empty. I slammed the cupboards open and closed with an anger I didn't recognise. Why did we never have any food? I loaded the dishwasher and stormed out of the flat. If Alex had been at home I know I'd have morphed into a hysterical rant. Why do I do it all? Why can't you help? Why isn't this a fifty–fifty deal? I'd have hated myself for asking those utterly predictable questions, but I'd have done it. We'd have been at war again, just as we were over our investments.

I splurged on a ready-cooked meal from Marks and Spencer and ate it alone in our kitchen. I didn't turn on the TV. I certainly didn't turn on our blasted Bloomberg terminal. I was in bed, alone, by nine. I'd never needed sleep so badly. But names like Bear Sterns and BNP Paribas haunted my dreams for the rest of that summer. They were in the news for all the wrong reasons back then.

All the gossip columns claim that City Boys take loads of recreational drugs in the good times. I believe they take more in the bad. When you're cold with fear even before you're fully awake, when your limbs won't move as the 5 a.m alarm goes off: that's when traders need help. When they end their days hollow and lost in some City bar: that's when they need distracting. Losing money – large amounts of money – arrests your mind. You can't concentrate. All night, all you can think about are the mistakes. Why did the market move that way? Why didn't you exit when you so desperately needed to?

The most worrying thing was that our oldest traders were looking ill. They were always so proud to have survived 1987's Black Monday and the Dot Com crisis. They clearly weren't surviving this one. Even Ollie was looking ruffled those days. I walked to the Tube with him one evening. 'Is it as bad as we think?' I asked as we parted. 'My dear, it's going to make every previous recession look like a bad hair day,' he said. What a wonderful but worrying phrase. I wondered briefly if he was on drugs himself. Nothing would have surprised me that summer.

With Roach and Gordon unusually quiet, other senior traders turned up the volume. About a dozen guys had huge blow-outs two days in a row, and they knew they were hanging on by a thread. Tommy, the trader closest to me, was handling the strain very oddly. He was talking incessantly at his monitors and the air around him. Was he on something? As it was, we simply tuned Tommy out. We were all waiting for a huge interest rate announcement from the European Central Bank and everyone was focused on clearing their order books before that time. But still, Tommy rambled on. When the ECB announced an unexpected cut, everyone panicked. It was far more than expected, and the bond markets soared immediately. So did Tommy. He screamed. Never has the same swear word been shouted so loud and so often. He was desperate to pull the order he'd accidently left in, but he didn't have time. His combined profits over the past four months disappeared in the split second of that ECB announcement. His losses were catastrophic – but more tragically, they were preventable, had he not been rambling like an idiot. He kicked his desk furiously, the desk behind him, the one next to him. He screamed as he grabbed one of the monitors on his desk. The cables held it firm so he couldn't lift or throw it and instead he kicked at his chair, driving it across the floor towards a colleague. Two traders beside him leaped in to stop him from doing any more damage. But in that moment he was still. He was broken. Then he threw a wild look around the office like a caged animal, and simply fled. He grabbed his jacket and gym bag and ran towards the lifts. Tommy was gone.

'How much is he down? How many orders did he have in?' We talked about little else that afternoon. The most credible rumour was that he'd lost as much as five million pounds of the boss's money in that one woeful mis-trade. No wonder he left so fast. Charlie and the boss would have sent him home in a Fed-Ex package if he'd stayed, and it was no surprise that none of us ever saw him again.

Sex got a lot of the boys through that long, painful summer. In my middle office job, affairs seemed to be the standard way to relieve the boredom. In the front office, one-night stands were the way to relieve market stress. Never had secretaries, HR staff, compliance and back office girls been in such high demand before the summer of 2007. Never had the meat markets of the Wharf or the City been so full. I wasn't exactly happy in my marriage at that point, but I was very glad I had a wedding ring on my finger. I just hoped Alex was wearing his. A lot of guys on my floor turned into walking clichés as they took theirs off before heading out into the night. Then they'd take some girl to a hotel room for a couple of hours before shelling out £250 for a late-night taxi back to Kent.

The most worrying thing of all for the wives and girl-friends – possibly myself included – was that the men didn't necessarily see that they had done anything wrong. I'm certain several could have passed lie detector tests saying they had never cheated on their wives. They may have physically cheated, but their minds had remained focused on the markets. To many, that emotional emptiness made it somewhat justifiable.

Our boss began paying more attention to us. He prowled the floor the way Charlie always had. He stood at our backs, watching everything and saying nothing. When the lay-offs began, I never found out if he did the dirty work, or if he had HR or some other depart-ment do it. People simply disappeared and never came back. Desks were cleared the following morning, just as they had been when Lisa had left, what felt like a hundred years earlier. There were no more wildly expensive Thursday night leaving drinks. After all, how could you have a whip round if you didn't know someone was leaving? In the past, everyone assumed that if the boss liked you, then you could lose every day for a month and he'd view it as a rough patch. On the other hand, if your face didn't fit, then you could get the chop after only a couple of days of losses. But nowadays, anyone could get the axe at any time. I averted my gaze away from those empty desks as I walked across the trading floor.

My heart felt heavy once again, and I developed an icy chill in the back of my throat each morning before the market opened. The volatility was getting more and more extreme. Market shocks – from central banks, Wall Street, anywhere, really – kept on coming. *What the hell is going on in the market*? I would literally let out cries of frustration some days as every single trade I put on turned against me. I felt lost and powerless, unable to comprehend the chaos around me.

Paranoia got to me as well. The knowledge that you were always on camera, that every keystroke was recorded, every phone conversation was logged and stored in case someone, somewhere, needed to invest-igate you gets to you after a while. It's a kind of an imprisonment within our wide-open trading floor. The empty desks merely served as a constant reminder of just how many of us had already been crushed.

Intraday trading had always involved a substantial amount of adrenaline, but sometimes it felt as if the rush could kill. Once, in the Ladies, I found myself standing by the mirror next to someone from Stella's team, a trader I'd seen but never spoken to. She was brutally honest about the effect that trading – particularly trading during the credit crisis – had on her. 'I've been sweating all morning,' she said, looking even more exhausted than myself. 'I could feel my shirt sticking to my back. My skirt felt as if it was steaming. I could have wrung my tights out in the sink here. It was never like this before.'

With those words she left me on my own to try and get my mind back into gear. What kind of environment was this? I simply couldn't remember why I had been so desperate to get into this world. Nor did I know when or how, I might be spat out. The colossal, soulless machine of the City was moving in directions that no one could predict or prevent. I was torn between a desire to tough it out and a sense that the time had already come to move on. I made a few enquiries about other jobs at other firms. Forget survival of the fittest. In the City it's more like survival of the fastest. If a new opportunity came up I wanted to be ready for it. I was not about to give it all up just yet.

# Chapter 14

REAL LIFE INTRUDED AND made the madness of City life even worse that summer 2007. Late one evening, I had a phone call from my mother. 'Suzana, I'm so sorry. Your grandmother has just died.' It was such a concise phrase. I'd adored my grandmother – a tough-as-nails Midwestern lady. I'm sure she could have been a Wall Street trader if her generation had allowed.

I flew home for her funeral but didn't cry. Then later, back in London, I couldn't stop. My legs felt eternally heavy as I forced myself out of bed each morning. Day after day, I found myself crying on the 6 a.m. tube into Canary Wharf, tears streaming down my face as I hid behind my *Financial Times* or squeezed behind a larger man in a suit. Even if anyone had noticed, no one would have said a word. Ignoring someone who is crying is normal behaviour for London commuters at that hour. With a coffee in my hand, I'd turn off my emotions and focus on trading. I would cry again in the Ladies around about midday. Those were the only times I was ever thankful that there were so few women in the City.

Bereavement and grief test a marriage. I think mine

was found wanting. Alex said all the right things. He appeared to be supportive straight after I heard the news, during the funeral and in all the grim, miserable days that followed. But for some reason, I felt it was all a sham, that he wasn't seeing me and he wasn't feeling it, that a computer could have delivered his words with more conviction. I slept alongside him every night but I had never felt so alone.

The distance was just as wide during the working day. Alex was only one office building away from me in Canary Wharf, but he may as well have been in a different world in 2007. His job was technical, theoretical, refined. He made more money than me, but he traded once a week, if that, and moreover, he didn't need to wring the sweat out of his clothes when he came home from work.

Nor did his body break down in the evenings that year. Mine did. I began to collapse the moment I got through the door. Sometimes I'd barely make it through the hall. I can honestly say that it baffled me – it wasn't as if I was doing extremely physical or dangerous work. But for some reason, I couldn't fight the toll the consistent stress ravaged on my system. I struggled to move once I'd hit our sofa at night. Sometimes I came home speechless, unable to cook, shop or clean. All I did was relive the horror of the day in the middle of our evening. I questioned my trades. I'd known what I was doing, I'd done it before. Why had it gone against me? Why was it so hard? I stopped going out during the week. The vibrant girl who had gone drinking with Roach,

Gordon and the gimps had become a robot. Staying up beyond ten was out of the question.

The blissful weekends away we'd had at the start of our relationship were nothing more than memories now. One of the side effects of the City is how many people become physically sick at weekends when their bodies react to the stress they have fought over the past five days. I lost weight, though I didn't have much to lose. I also wanted to scream when I got home and found Alex trading in our flat. Making money was still a game to him. It was a challenge, not a battle for survival. The markets began to haunt me, sapping every last piece of energy. But still it roared ahead frenetically, the lifeblood behind millions of graphs and figures and jobs, stresses and sorrows, winners and losers. With the markets not only pervading my office but also my home, there was room for little else – it was omnipotent – markets, markets, markets, twenty-four seven. How much can one person absorb? Was this the world I'd been so desperate to break into when I'd started off in the City? I'd been thrilled by it a year ago, now it was suffocating me. Trading had become an obsession – and a trap. Had I ever had a life beyond analysing the market into oblivion? Did I know anyone who didn't obsess over the latest MPC rate cuts or the non-farm payroll figures? Everyone I spent time with – mostly City bankers – had a commitment to their jobs that bordered on psychosis. I could no longer talk about the cinema, because I was too exhausted to go. I had my music degree, of course, but at that point I was as likely to go to a music recital as I was to go to Basra. I may have physically lived in the fantastically central and cosmopolitan Bayswater, but my psyche remained trapped within the glass and steel skyscrapers of Canary Wharf long after I returned home at night. I went back to Canary Wharf in my dreams, but increasingly, it had become the stuff of my nightmares.

'We've got to start going out again. We used to have so much fun,' Alex would say. I knew what he meant. I couldn't work out how our lives had changed so much in only a year. When it came to relationships, the credit crunch was clearly a cancer, not a tidal wave. It could seep through any couple's defences. At work I'd listen in as Roach or Gordon hung up on, or shouted at, their wives and girlfriends. They simply wouldn't – couldn't – talk to them while their trades were haemorrhaging. Then, instead of going home to the one person in the world who actually cared, the guys hit the bars, sinking into belligerence with the other Wharf-heads. It was an ugly, stupid, self-destructive pattern. Was I in danger of tracing it out myself? No, I would salvage my marriage, I vowed one day as Roach refused to take his wife's call yet again. Somehow I will find the energy to be me again.

I began by being honest with Charlie. I felt he was one person I could trust. I spoke to him in a quiet corner of our coffee room just after seven. 'I know you don't like us bringing any personal issues into the office,' I began. 'But recently I have lost someone in my family. I'm struggling to cope with that. My marriage is also on the rocks, maybe like all our marriages. I don't know why, but I felt you should know all this.'

'I'd be upset too,' he admitted, candidly. 'Have you taken any holiday lately?'

'I've taken enough. And I don't need more. Working here drives me mad, but it keeps me sane as well. I don't quite know how that works, but it's true.' We drank our coffees in silence for a while. Charlie didn't pry into the details. He asked if there was anything else the company could do which, of course, there wasn't. He checked I wanted to carry on as normal, and I did.

Then we went back upstairs and he cut my trading limits.

I like to believe he did it out of kindness. I like to think he felt he was saving me from myself. But I couldn't help being gigantically pissed-off. Lowering your limits restricts you from making big profits. But who amongst us was doing that during the summer? The positive spin of lower limits is lower potential losses. If your limits are cut in half after a big loss, it can take twice as long to earn your money back. But if lower limits take the pressure off, then you're more likely to trade well. It's the whole tortoise and hare thing – and, as usual, Charlie turned out to have played it just right. Mistakes were less expensive on my new trading limits. So I made fewer of them. The anger helped me focus my mind on winning again. Charlie had given me a new point to prove; he knew that was the best way to motivate me.

I staggered through July and August. I was up at five, at my desk long before seven, and still reliving trades in my head long after the market closed. I made a little, lost a little, fought a lot.

I was able to pick up the pace at home as well. I forced myself to cook, and tried to plan interesting excursions at the weekend. I begged Alex to take us out to the country on the bike on Sundays. The City seemed so far away when we were sitting in the garden of some English country pub. A change of scene really did put things in perspective. I could suddenly see why so many of my colleagues lived in Kent or Essex or beyond. The last thing you wanted on a weekend was to turn a corner and see Tower 42, the Gherkin, or the Wharf.

I had some laughs in the office as well. A bit of banter did wonders. When we laughed, I remembered why I was there. When I relaxed, I remembered that it felt even better to win. I wanted to lighten up. I wanted to feel that the whole credit crisis was just a phase, a summer storm like the one that had greeted me on my very first day in the City. I wanted to believe it would be over just as quickly.

The big boss put paid to that. One day in late August he called all the traders to the floor for a meeting after the market closed. It began at 4 p.m. sharp, and we congregated in a room warmed by the glistening sun. The Thames was a glittering coil of silver in the early afternoon glow, and the commuter boats and barges that take out so much of the capital's rubbish left criss-crossing marks on the water. Planes departing City Airport left white patterns across the sky. Life was carrying on as normal in the outside world, it was only within these glass and concrete towers that everything had changed.

As our boss requested silence, I realised it was pretty much the first time I had ever heard him speak. Whenever he stood behind my desk studying my trades, he was silent. I'd never known if that was good or bad. It turned out he had a strong, very deep voice and an extraordinarily colourful choice of words. What he didn't appear to have, was a sense of humour. This was not a man who cared about being liked – which was probably part of the reason he had done so well for so long in the bear pit of finance.

He began discussing those 'external forces' that ate into our profits. What profits would those be, exactly? We were losing money day in and day out. He talked of 'dark forces at play', then began to lay into hedge funds. We relished this, because we all hated them too. Several of the world's largest and most ruthless funds created computer algorithms that could see when we entered into our spread trades. Those same funds could then move the market against us, and turn a profit for themselves, buying back the positions we had taken for less after we'd sold at a loss. 'If any of you sometimes feel like you're being watched it's because, well, you are,' the boss said.

He went on to state that, in his opinion, market manipulation went further. The big hedge funds were regularly placing big, false bids that could fool traders like us into inappropriate positions. Algorithmic trading systems, designed by the world's brightest PhD students, would always have the upper hand over our faux-news reliant, instinctive style of business. There's an old City line: the economy depends on economists about as much as the weather depends on weather forecasters. Were our instincts not as useless as weathermen?

'Does anyone have any good ideas?' our boss asked, seeking acumen. We all stood in silence – an embarrassing silence that felt as if it lasted a lifetime.

'If the boss is that panicky, you want to start sending your CV out,' Roach whispered as we headed back to the floor.

'I'm already on it,' I said. It was only half a joke. I don't know why, but I'd updated it at home the day after David quit with stress. 'Just in case,' I'd said to Alex at the time. Perhaps it was time to press 'send'.

Three days later, I lost a million pounds. The Dow Jones had crashed for five days in a row and for all the talk of the ubiquitous hedge funds, two of the world's largest had just gone spectacularly bust – and there were rumours that several more would fail in the next few weeks. No one knew what the implications of all that was.

It was one of the market's most chaotic days. We weren't just staring at our monitors and scrambling for market gossip via internet and phone. We moved around the floor in a pack, gathered around one desk after another, chasing each new theory and each rubbish piece of information.

'What's going on?' I asked as we assembled near Tobias. No one knew and, for once, this wasn't a case of trader secrecy. It wasn't the senior traders protecting their positions and pushing us all into our boxes. No one did know. That was the problem.

Instead, I focused on the eye of the storm. I returned to my desk, devouring information, and then took a position. I convinced myself I wasn't going to be 'long and wrong'. I had faith, and I bet big. But it didn't go according to plan.

'Oh please, no. Oh dear God, no.' My monitors flashed up an increasingly disastrous mess. This trade was a huge, dreadful mistake. The back of my throat clenched, and my breathing accelerated as I simply dug myself a massive financial hole. I focused, trying to calm my whole metabolism. But every minute was more catastrophic than the last. Every tick was going against me. I adopted a stony, cold silence. I said my prayers and tried not to look at the clock. I needed time, but I feared it as well. And I was so far offside! Time to act. Can I double up again? Is there time? An hour ago I'd been facing what felt like heart-stopping losses of £200,000. Now I was so much deeper in the shit. My breathing – what was happening to my breathing? I was at my stop loss, the worst-case scenario, an unimaginably bad, career-ending place. I had to cut my losses, but with amounts this large, I simply couldn't. For once in my trading career, I froze. Amidst the madness of that terrible office my brain was screaming, 'Quit!' My hand was on my mouse. The cursor was blinking on my monitor. All I had to do was click. But I couldn't. For reasons I could never understand, I froze.

'Suzana, get out of there!'

It was Charlie. He shouldered me out of my own chair. It swung round fast, bashing my knees against the drawers of my desk, tipping me into the aisle. Charlie was taking over. I saw him grab my mouse. He lined up the cursor. Then he hit market and did what he had to do – what I should have done. My devastating losses became crystallised in that moment.

I couldn't speak, or look at Charlie. How many others were watching? I don't think anyone on the floor could have missed what had just happened. I have no idea how I made it across the floor to the toilets. There, I was physically sick. Blood was thumping through my ears. The sound of Charlie's voice was in my head. 'Suzana, get out of there.' It echoed inside my head – the swing of the chair, the sense of being watched, the enormity of my losses. I moved towards the row of three sinks. Who was that shattered, awful-looking girl in the mirror? Why was she so pale? What had happened to her?

The last time I registered steep losses, I pulled myself together relatively fast. Not today. I just walked back to my desk without brushing my hair. For once, it didn't matter. I still looked like a million dollars compared to the guys. Everyone took a hit that day, and the turbulence continued every day for the rest of that week.

Our company took massive, sustained losses. And the office furniture took massive, sustained damage.

The one thing I could never explain to my family and my few remaining non-City friends was how I could lose a million pounds and not lose my job. One explanation is simple: I hadn't lost the money because of a mistake, a weakness, or some act of gross misconduct. I'd got caught out by the markets – just like everyone else had. The other answer is more complex. London's long, murky past includes a lot of unsavoury episodes. When the City buys you, it owns you. It's pseudo blackmail. Now I'd lost so much that, to my bank, I was effectively an indentured slave. I was supposed to be grateful. Ideally, the company would have me stay just as long as it took to earn it all back. Could I, though?

Perhaps. But Charlie and Roach taught me one crucial thing: that the world's best investors know when to sell. This translated to other areas of life: as an employee, I needed to know when to leave my company. I also had to leave on my own terms.

In late 2007, I was fed up with fighting the fear pervading those silver escalators inside Canary Wharf Tube each morning. I didn't enjoy witnessing the exhaustion on my colleagues' faces each evening. We weren't saving lives. We weren't risking our own skins. We shouldn't be getting so old, so fast, in that isolated trading room. It was absurd to expend so much energy on something that wasn't there if you closed your eyes.

I kept my head down and built my limits back up as anxious savers began queuing up for their money outside Northern Rock branches and the whole system looked set to crash. I carried on trading as interest rates were slashed in both the United States and Europe, and banks from Wall Street to Switzerland went bust. Day after day, I began to replace at least a fraction of the cash I had lost. But in the meantime, I secured a series of interviews elsewhere.

'There's nothing out there. Bankers are extinct. It's over,' I was told by one ferocious head-hunter. 'I should tell you that the number of CVs on my desk has gone up 450 per cent in six months,' said another.

'Well, can you put mine at the top of the pile?' I asked. 'I'll consider almost anything. Just get me out of Canary Wharf.'

# Chapter 15

I WAS IN A time-warp and life became just a little bit surreal. My head-hunter found me an interview – quite possibly the last interview any City banker got that year. 'It's for a derivatives trading firm,' he'd said, at the start of a very long, complex job description. I was barely listening.

'Is it in Canary Wharf?' was all I asked when he was done.

'It's in Mayfair.'

'Sounds great.'

For the first interview I wore my favourite Loro Piana suit. It was very body-hugging, but revealed absolutely no skin. I took a taxi to Berkeley Square and walked through some of London's most luxurious streets. This used to be where the City boys and I came to party in the good times. Hopefully, I could get a job here in the bad. It was mid-morning, and doormen were busy polishing jet-black railings and shiny gold door fittings. Bentleys and Lamborghinis zoomed past with blacked-out windows and personalised plates. I thought of Martin, previously so determined to get his £100k licence plate, who now simply worried about not getting fired. Those sort of everyday worries didn't seem to concern life in W1. The neighbourhood oozed old money, effortless power and stability. Ironically, it was the latter that attracted me the most. In Mayfair, in 2007, the credit crunch was still, to many, a media exaggeration. Best not be mentioned, lest it excite the staff. How I wanted to pretend that was true.

If they offered me the job, my new office would be located in a Georgian townhouse, home of a rich merchant banker and his family nearly three hundred years ago. The door was foreboding and sophisticated. There was a heavy oak desk in the atrium, and a receptionist so polite he practically doffed his cap – even though he wasn't wearing one. I signed in and was greeted a by a plump middle-aged lady who resembled a socialite in her camel-tweed suit. She led me up the wide staircase, past a wall of what looked like Old Masters paintings. The first room I walked through was extremely hushed, yet fully staffed. There were only a few computers on the desks, and I felt it was a little like being on a film set for a Sunday night costume drama.

This impression grew in the actual interview. The man I was there to meet was about sixty years old and talked with the English reticence of Alfred Hitchcock. I realised at this point I'd infiltrated the 'old City'. I sold them my trading prowess, my youthful injection of energy and, even though they didn't have a single American in their blue-blooded firm (and hated dissenters), I had the advantage of being the least 'American' American person they'd ever come across. This was going to be an extreme move,

I thought to myself. But anything extreme, at that point, was good.

His office was furnished with mahogany, leather-topped desks and gilt-framed landscapes. Less than an hour earlier, I was on the trading floor in my testosterone-fuelled, twenty-first-century office block. This place, conversely, was a glimpse into a bygone era.

Initially, my Hitchcock lookalike was benevolently charming. He appeared genuinely interested in my taxi ride to the office. He also seemed desperately keen to know whether I was enjoying the abnormally sunny weather. He smiled warmly through the small talk as we waited for coffee to be served. Then came my wake-up call. We got down to business, and the grilling intensified. Looking back, I cannot say how much I respected him from that moment on. He was fierce, but fair. He described his firm's business in concise, clinical detail. No showboating, no exaggeration, just a sober account of the age-old business of making money and serving billionaire West End clients. Then he began with the interrogation. Over the course of ninety minutes, he extracted every residue of information I possessed about derivatives. He tested my knowledge on every trend, strategy, and quirk of over-the-counter markets. He led me through the City, peppering me with questions. If I hadn't been so intent on impressing him, I would have been shocked. This harmless-looking, sixty-something man was actually quite fierce, and I regret that I hadn't seen that from the start. City girls, of all people, should know that appearances can be deceptive.

'I do hope we will be seeing you again,' he said when my ordeal was over.

He did. I needed to schedule another 'dental appointment' three days later when I was called back. That day, I had a panel interview in a Merchant Ivory-style boardroom. I sat down on a skilfully carved chair at a table so elegant I was afraid to touch it. My interrogators were unpredictable: a tough-looking woman in her fifties, a girl in her early thirties and a man of about forty. In all my City years, I don't think I'd ever been in a room where the men were in the minority. I certainly hadn't expected it to occur inside the old-school ties of Mayfair. 'We only hire the best,' said the woman at the end of my interview. Was that a threat, a challenge or a compliment? I simply couldn't tell.

A week later, I discovered that the comment must have been a seal of approval. I was called back to see Alfred Hitchcock. Again, he was briefly fascinated by the details of my taxi ride and thoughts on the weather. Then he offered me the job, and opened a drawer behind him, which revealed a bottle of whisky and what looked like cut-crystal glasses. This place would never stop surprising me. 'You will be aware, young lady, that we do things differently here,' he said as the ice cubes in his glass clinked together. 'I do hope you will enjoy the contrast.'

I resigned before the market opened the next morning. It was the first time I'd actually been inside my billionaire boss's corner office. He leaned over an enormous, opaque glass desk enveloped by modern art on three of the four walls, and he wouldn't even turn down the volume of *CNBC* for our first – and last – conversation. 'That's too bad,' he declared as I handed over my resignation letter. 'We thought you had potential. Charlie always thought you were the dark horse.' While I'm not exactly sure what that meant, I knew I could walk away with my pride intact. Yes, I'd lost big-time the previous month. No, I'd not yet come close to recouping that amount of money – not this year, anyway. But I worked out that my previous gains easily cancelled out the losses of that one terrible day. I was ahead on points. It was time to go.

I turned in my security pass and left the building. I headed home, got changed and returned to the Wharf when the markets closed, as I didn't want this to end without buying Roach, Gordon, Tobias and some of the others a drink. But when the evening came, it was the most uninspired leaving do I can recall. For the traders I left behind, morale was extremely low. The ship was sinking and I was the rat.

It wasn't even seven o'clock when I descended into Canary Wharf underground station for the very last time. I would miss the boys, but not the brutality. Time to try and make it elsewhere.

My new firm presented a learning curve so steep it was almost back-breaking. Every day, the contrasts in my new, strikingly traditional, office amazed me. Computers and technology were trivialised in their world, and it was only the young, female secretaries who really relied on the screens in front of them. Many of the men appeared to just work with paper files. I absorbed this in shock. If this wasn't a dangerous anachronism, then it was unquestionably a fire risk. My desk was situated in a room of approximately twenty-five consultants. Those Mayfair office blocks really are like the Tardis – far larger inside than they look. I was given a lot of reading to complete during my first morning, and it felt appropriate in a room that resembled a library. At first, the stillness was off-putting. Is that man asleep? Is anyone here aware that there's a financial crisis going on outside? They were, of course. I wasn't listening to the sound of silence in Mayfair. I was listening to the sound of old money at work. The rich, at this level, did things very differently indeed.

Still, for all the grey in their hair, my new colleagues had a youthful glint in their eyes that hinted at incredibly bright minds behind their wrinkled façades. What fascinated me most about my new, sheltered City bank is that for all the money people were making, no one really needed to work – most were born into the poshest families in London, Europe and beyond. They wanted a cosy office and nice title, and had no idea what real passion was. I missed my old circus almost immediately.

At noon a girl approached me, she was roughly my age. She was wearing thick black tights, a black miniskirt, and a tight, dark woollen sweater – a beacon of cool in a sea of tweed. I hoped we'd hit it off immediately. 'I'm Lauren,' she said. 'I'm going to be walking you through the ropes.' She sat next to me for several hours a day for the next twelve weeks, and was, without a doubt, one of the most brilliant girls I'd ever met. Mensa would probably need a new category for Lauren. It seemed there was no investment complexity she couldn't break down, no product she couldn't analyse or understand. The worrying thing was that my job was to do the same. I was there to price, trade and consult on several different types of over-the-counter derivatives – instruments that were fast becoming the ugliest buzz words of the credit crunch. They were, according to Warren Buffett, 'financial weapons of mass destruction' that everyone had come to hate and fear in equal measure.

At their simplest, derivatives are instruments that allow investors to speculate on the future price of, for example, commodities such as sugar or wheat or shares – without buying the underlying investment. They can generate earnings that are often wildly overstated and based on estimates whose inaccuracy may not be revealed for years. Derivatives, like futures, options and swaps, were developed to allow investors to hedge their risks in financial markets – in effect, buying insurance against market movements – but quickly became a means of investment in their own right. They've grown exponentially over the last twenty years into a multi-trillion-dollar industry – indeed, OTC derivatives contracts – excluding those traded on exchanges such as the International Petroleum Exchange – are now worth close to eighty-five trillion dollars.

Buffett declared that the derivatives business was like hell: easy to enter, but almost impossible to leave. His view was that the most complex derivatives appeared to have been developed by madmen – the kind of instruments Lauren and I analysed every day.

'So what exactly are you doing?' my mother would ask on the phone. She'd understood crunching numbers in my first City jobs, and intraday trading in my second. But how to explain this? 'Well, today I deconstructed a swap with six binary options, several floors and caps underneath. I also looked at foreign exchange options, participating forwards, exotic options, outstanding contracts, and hedging strategies for our clients. Hello? Mum, are you there?' In the end I went for phrases like: 'It's complicated but I'm really just getting to grips with the way the business works.' I'm just glad my mother didn't ask me what I was finding out.

Two things became clear early on. The first was that many bankers deserved every bit of the criticism that was already being thrown at them by the public. As we analysed portfolios, it was possible to see what had been going on inside people's heads as the credit crunch got underway. The real players saw that the Gilded Age was coming to an end, and they planned accordingly, milking the system for every penny they could get. Out there everyone's long-term interests were being sacrificed for the very short-term financial gain of the very few, morally bankrupt elite.

Another realisation was that many fund managers were as clueless about market developments as their burned-out investors. In the boom times, stories circulated about how analysts were employed simply to add pages of calculations to their valuation systems. All the extra sums just took the final figure back to where it would have been without them. So why were the analysts there, exactly? New, clever and complicated things had to be good, right? As I continued to restructure those rather destructive derivatives, the ethos of a typical City banker reverberated loudly in the back of my mind: 'As long as the storm doesn't hit till I've got one last bonus and got out – who gives a damn?' This was, supposedly, everyone's exit strategy.

It was quite refreshing to finally see the truth of how the public had been taken for one over-extended credit holiday over the past few decades. Bankers stopped banking and became magicians, using misdirection, deception and illusion to make their billions. What's securitisation, after all, if not a hoax? Is it any different from the age-old trick where the magician turns a penny in one hand into a pound coin? In the City, bankers took sub-prime mortgages, sold them to investors all over the world and distanced the lender from the borrower so far that the penny loan really did look like a one-pound one. The investors – and the regulators – could not believe their eyes and could not think of an explanation for the astronomical profits. Pure magic.

My job was to get wise to what the market was doing. That way the firm's clients could be protected from the worst excesses of the system. Lauren and I had to be the early warning system, checking through all the things modern-day cowboys had hidden far from their balance sheets. This kind of deception meant all sorts of toxic debts could be shielded from view. It could change a firm's P&L from red to green, just like magicians change the colour of a silk handkerchief. They didn't even need a magic wand. Speed was an easy tool to fool as well. By innovating financial products at a mind-boggling pace, bankers overwhelmed the capacity of both the regulators and the financial institutions themselves to assess the risk. They don't call it 'pulling a fast one' for nothing, right?

'It's ugly stuff,' I'd say to Lauren, day after day as we identified yet more potentially dangerous investments floating around the markets.

Lauren's encouragement helped me thrive in Mayfair. She took time to nurture my strengths, and to iron out my weaknesses. After the sink or swim environment I'd left behind, it was unspeakably great to feel looked after. But while I was probably the least technical person the company had ever employed, Mr Hitchcock astutely spotted that I liked a challenge, and I had skills the others lacked. I kept my head down, learning from my stylish new mentor and studying for my next set of professional exams – the FSA. Contrary to the pressures of the Eurex, I breezed through the FSA exams, free from the manic rush of intraday trading. In my new role, I worried instead about what I might have missed. But the more complex derivatives became, the more hazardous they were, as liquidity dried up rapidly in early 2008. My job was to make sure they didn't burst before our investors took cover.

Tobias emailed me months after I left. He too had quit the bank. I returned to the Wharf for his leaving drinks, and it was a distressing evening. The boys looked old, their faces looked downtrodden by the demands of trading life.

'So, how do we compare to your new colleagues?' someone asked me early on. 'What's your new place like?'

'It's like you're from a different planet. You know the feeling you get when you get out of a sauna and into an ice-cold plunge pool? That's the difference.

'As far as the personalities are concerned, I've gone from cowboy traders to borderline autistic maths geniuses,' I said. The boys were thrilled that I missed them.

Tobias was the real surprise that night. He wasn't heading west like me. He was leaving the City altogether. 'I'm going back to Norway to be a maths teacher.'

'I'm not sure the City will survive without you, but if it's what you want . . .' I told him as we said goodbye. The following morning I imagined him in smart, functional clothes at a school in some pristine Nordic village.

He seemed happy with his decision. After all, everyone looked happier when they escaped the confines of Canary Wharf. Over the past few months, I certainly rediscovered something that proprietary trading had managed to take from me – quality of life. In Mayfair, I didn't need to be at my desk till the more humane hour of 9 a.m. Better still, I walked to work down some of London's loveliest streets. Along the way, I would encounter a cornucopia cross-section of people who lived radically different lives. On those God-awful 6 a.m. Jubilee lines to Canary Wharf, the only people I ever saw were rival City workers or cleaners. The City, in those early morning hours was so deranged and polarised, it was as if the only people who exist are those at the very top or the very bottom of the social pecking order. No wonder everyone's values got so screwed up. In my new job, I actually had time to take lunch. I sat outside in Berkeley Square or in Green Park when the weather was lovely. Unfortunately, the walk home was the one bit of the day that the old butter-flies began to resurface. That meant seeing Alex and facing up to the true state of our marriage. Deconstructing swaps was much more palatable – and that's not something people say every day.

When I left Canary Wharf, I was convinced that my new job would give us a fresh start. I would be able to relax a bit when I wasn't intraday trading. If I wasn't so strained, exhausted or empty, then we could go back to where we'd started. I could be the girl with the big dreams and he could be the guy with even bigger ones.

Perhaps you can't turn back time, however. Alex just didn't seem interested when I tried to describe my new colleagues to him. Was he actually jealous that I'd escaped from my old bank just before the City's shutters came down for good? I knew his firm was struggling and his relatively stress-free role had become a hell of a lot tougher. I could sense he was haunted by some of my old fears when the markets went against him. What I couldn't do was get him to open up about it. And fighting so many sex wars at work, it now seemed I had to face them at home as well. His former, minor contributions to our domestic life were essentially abandoned. What was it that the dynamic American banker had said at my first-ever 'Women in the City' networking event? 'Even if you do break through the glass ceiling, you'll still be expected to pick up the glass.' I did too much tidying up in the first few months of my new job and I knew something had to give. I just didn't know what or how.

Mayfair was home to more than a few capable and powerful women. Meeting some of them was a revelation. A few months into my job I was at a networking event and met a lady who worked for a similar derivatives trading company just one gilded street away. Her name was Frances and she was the only female partner her firm had, or had ever had. She was a tall, angular creature and we had a wonderful chat about the past over drinks that first evening. If I thought I'd had it hard in Canary Wharf I only needed to listen to my new friend for some perspective. Apparently the Council of the Stock Exchange hadn't decided to admit women to its hallowed halls until 1968. Even then, it had a struggle on its hands. The Council had recommended a vote in favour of the motion and a recommendation, in those days, was effectively an instruction. But the City Boys ignored it. When the count came in, there were 663 votes in favour of the change and 1,366 against. They eventually allowed women in in subsequent years, but by the time Frances joined the City, in the 1970s, women were still barred from certain pubs and restaurants. Professional associations, clubs and private dining rooms – where the real deals were done – were all off-limits for women. But Frances had battled through. She had fought the system for more than three decades – and the battle had clearly taken its toll. We met for coffee every now and then and I occasionally sensed elements of real sadness about her. She was married, but she'd never had time for children. She never drank, and she *never* let her guard down. I thought of how poorly behaved the boys were in Canary Wharf, and the long, very boozy lunches the older men had in Mayfair. They didn't have to watch their step. It hadn't been the same for Frances – she needed to behave impeccably every day. She'd learned, long ago, not to rock any boats, to go with the flow. She had long, presumably lovely hair, but I don't think her colleagues ever got to see it; she tied it back in a

241

tight, unattractive bun every day. She played down her femininity, deliberately making herself look as plain as possible, merging into the dark woods of her office with her sobering blacks, dark blues and greys. Oh, and her key message every time we met was that women must never – and I mean *never* – make mistakes.

Fortunately, the younger girls back in my office were a little less inhibited. Yes, we had our basic City uniform of Oxford shirts and suits. Yes, we kept the accessories muted and didn't turn too many heads. But at least, unlike City Girls of the past, we were treated as equals. Or at least, that's what I thought at first. It was the late spring of 2008 when I began to see another difficult and unpleasant truth.

My new role involved a lot more client contact. We had to speculate to accumulate in those tough times and we needed to keep our existing customers sweet and continue getting new ones through our doors. I was looking forward to playing my part, after all, I was always up for a trip outside the office. I could deconstruct a swap later.

'Suzana, we'd like you to join Marcus for a briefing in the City at eleven tomorrow morning,' I was told. Marcus was one of our old timers, a nice white-haired guy in his mid- to late-fifties. There was a whiff of my former colleague Ollie about him. I doubt he'd ever really been young, so to speak, and I was happy to be on his team. We were travelling to an office near Liverpool Street to update a client on market developments and future hedging prospects. Marcus told me more about them in the taxi. I may have been the junior partner, but I felt like an equal as we rode the lift to the twenty-second floor. Once there, we were led to a boardroom. Three men greeted us. There were handshakes all round and all five of us sat down. A lady came in with a tray of tea, coffee and biscuits. She placed it on a table in the corner and left. No one moved. Our small talk went on and I realised I was desperate for a drink. So were the others, judging by their furtive glances at the coffee tray. So why was no one offering refreshments? The answer hit me out of nowhere. This was their office. I was their guest. But they were waiting for me to get up and serve. They really were. Marcus began his presentation and I tried to focus. I said a few things myself but I could sense I annoyed or even disappointed my colleague. Our three hosts, all very charming when I had been introduced, seemed to be cooling by the moment. It was as if a battle of wills had been played out – and it wasn't clear who had won.

Our meeting lasted about forty-five minutes. We covered a lot of ground. I was asked to explain several of the complexities of the products we advised upon and I had no problem with the explanations and happily tackled all the follow-up questions. I felt good, in total control of my brief. But the mood, when we left, was slightly less than jovial. The untouched coffee jugs must have been stone cold.

'Well, thank God you didn't get up,' Lauren said when I told her all about it later that afternoon.

'So you don't think I was imagining it?'

'Not at all. Margaret Thatcher could have been in that meeting and they'd have wanted her to play mother. They drive me mad sometimes.'

'So they're always like this?'

'They can't help themselves. I met Marcus in the City for a meeting once and I wasn't sure where the office was. "Come out on to Threadneedle Street then go north, north-west for about a minute and you'll be there," he said. What the hell is north, north-west? In the labyrinthine City streets . . . Please? Do I look like a Boy Scout?'

We carried on laughing over a few bottles of wine in Shepherd's Market that night. Two of our other colleagues joined us. Heather, who worked on the floor above and Gary, who had recently joined the firm and sat three desks from me.

'I've been telling Suzana about the old timers and how infuriating they can be,' Lauren began. Heather leaped in with plenty of stories of her own. Her favourite was the time she and Marcus had entertained some clients at Wimbledon.

'We'd had a lovely day and I think we'd actually won some decent new business so everyone was happy,' she said. 'Then the best bit came on the way home. We got into one of the shared taxis they lay on to get you back to the Tube and I'd sat next to Marcus on the back seat. A smartly dressed woman I'd have put in her mid-twenties was on the pull-down seat in front.

Marcus got talking to her and when she said she worked at Wimbledon he asked if she was a ball girl. It turned out she ran the website. It was mortifying and thank God she was game enough to laugh about it.'

'He's a lovely man but he's from another age,' Lauren said when we'd stopped laughing. Things sobered up a bit after that. Put four City workers around a table in the early summer of 2008 and the jokes soon started to wear thin. However much we might want to talk about other things we always ended up going back to the state of the market. My argument was that the regulators, the government, everyone involved in keeping the ship afloat was still in denial about the scale of the problem. They focused on their narrow little world of deals and never looked below the waterline. I knew that Jason and some of my other former colleagues from the back and middle offices could have pointed out some icebergs if they'd been given the chance to actually talk to the traders. Building up all those walls between different teams and different offices had been a disaster. Running the City like a caste system where those at the top never deign to speak to those below had been a fundamental weakness. 'Everyone in the City needs to get out of their comfort zone and meet other people,' I said when our conversation moved on – as it nearly always did – to the way we'd improve things given a chance. 'There are eyes and ears at every level in every company but no one takes advantage of them. We all work in our own little closed worlds. No wonder hardly anyone knows what's going on or what's going to happen next.'

It's hard to end an evening on a good note when the conversation always runs back to the credit crunch. We talked markets for the rest of the night and our little group broke up when the bar closed around midnight. After all my years of 5.30 a.m. alarm calls and 7 a.m. starts I still got a kick out of being able to stay out so late and not give a damn. 'Let's all change the world tomorrow,' Heather called out as we all parted. I smiled as I headed home. The culture of the City was never going to change overnight. But it was going to change – and I wanted a front row seat when it did.

# Chapter 16

MEETING CLIENTS WAS MY salvation for the rest of the year. The more people I spoke to the more enthusiastic I got about the industry. No one could ignore our problems and everyone had different ideas about how to solve them. My best moments came when some boardroom full of older, grey-haired men finally gave me their full attention. I'd got used to being paired up with Marcus or some of our other old-timers and I could sense that some of our clients expected me to take on the role of the eager to learn graduate trainee or, worse, the dutiful daughter. I loved that split second when they realised I might actually have seen more of the industry than them. I'd talk about what their compliance teams were no doubt doing that very day. I'd say how the markets would look to the supervisors in their middle offices. Then I'd have something to say about my own time on the trading floor.

'I think we've impressed them, my dear,' Marcus would remark after some of our most productive meetings. But I'd be lying if I said they all went well. There were still times when I couldn't get my message across or overcome our hosts' preconceptions. There were times when our clients seemed to bristle at my very presence. 'We need to watch our language, chaps, remember there's a young lady present,' a board member said one long, depressing afternoon. I had the feeling that the whole dynamic of that meeting had changed merely because I was there. They had modified their behaviour. I didn't learn a thing from them – and as far as I was concerned not learning was the worst crime of all. Making a fuss after a few bad meetings was out of the question. This was no time to rock the boat.

In 2008, an already tight City job market was tightening still further. The year began with global markets recording their biggest falls since 9/11. And it kept getting worse. Interest rates were slashed faster than any time in a generation. Some of the world's oldest, most established companies were falling by the wayside. 'Who's next?' was the only question anyone asked. That and: 'Just how bad can it get?' It was particularly worrying that the older, supposedly wiser heads around me in Mayfair couldn't supply answers. But as investment theory dictates, past performance is no guarantee of future results. We could have employed someone who'd personally watched the 1929 Wall Street Crash, and I don't believe he could have dealt with the 2008 version. What bothered me most about my older colleagues' faces wasn't that this was the worst environment they'd seen in decades – it was that it was the worst they'd seen, ever. Our strategy meetings became increasingly tense, just as they had on the Wharf before I quit. We were supposed to innovate new and improved

recommendations, trading strategies, hedging requirements: anything to see us through the fog. But fewer
and fewer of us ever had anything to say. The sound
of silence in Mayfair was even more frightening than
the cry of anger in Canary Wharf.

Between my City friends, the fears kept growing as
well. An old friend from another bank came round for
dinner one night. He offered up a very worrying example
of just how much denial everyone was in. He discussed
the two ways his firm utilised valuing its trading book.
'We drew up two different financial models to give an
idea of where we stood. The first showed us breaking
even – which was, admittedly, a huge worry as we'd
been making more than a hundred million the previous
year. The second showed us taking a £400 million hit
to our bottom line. Our MD had to choose which one
to use when he provided our quarterly results.'

'Do we even need to guess?' I asked.

'No you don't. He buried the loss and told the world
we're on course for a respectable break-even value.'

'That's terrifying.'

'It's not even the half of it. The models were designed
to work out how much our maximum loss was likely
to be. But neither of them took into account counter-
party risk, or worst-case scenarios. God knows how
low the true figure could be.'

I picked up the pace on my morning march to work
after hearing news like that. The weather was warmer,
but the chill from the City had finally infected robust
Mayfair. So much for the dull stability of my new job.

The butterflies returned to my stomach some days. I had a vulnerable feeling as I spent another day examining instruments and indices on models that no longer worked the way anyone expected. We hired a nice young guy a few weeks earlier. I'd sat in on his interview, but we had already let him go, partially for failing to perform to a sufficient level, but mainly because we no longer had anything for him to do. Most clients, at this stage, were too scared to invest in anything but cash. Others had shut up shop. In the office everyone looked pale, anxious and worked more frantically than usual. It was just like Canary Wharf, and the financial news was getting worse by the day. The new guy was the first to be let go, in a kind of 'last in, first out', rule that many banks operate under, but he clearly wasn't going to be the last. When would our cull begin? Which of us would be the next to be voted off this privileged little island?

The company's initial response to the slump was to try and woo and cajole our remaining clients into action. It wasn't easy. Several had billions and billions of pounds on deposit, ready to invest when they thought the market was bottoming out. Our job was to encourage the clients that the time had come to lay down their money despite their fears. With crude at $150 a barrel, inflation was still far higher than the Bank of England desired, and as we faced unprecedented market illiquidity and dislocation between LIBOR and base rates, confusion spread like wildfire. It was no surprise that the big players sat on their hands and wallets. But no deals meant no need for our expensive advice. Our charm-offensive became increasingly desperate. 'We're here if you need us,' we would say as we shook hands and left yet another boardroom empty-handed. In the meantime, we balanced the books with plenty of distressed debt deals and a lot of restructuring operations. It became a big deal when we closed a new deal. I sometimes traded less than once a week. It seemed comical as I thought back to the trading madness I performed less than a year prior to this. We now moved on geological time, and it would take ages to change course or find a new strategy.

With so little going on in the markets, it was little wonder that champagne sales were quite low in the late 2008 bonus season. I wasn't expecting much this year, as I'd only just joined. But with markets this grim, I didn't think anyone else in the company would be celebrating much either. Or would they?

Lauren and Heather got bit of a group together to talk about our bonuses shortly after they were paid. It was a little like the discussions I'd had with Roach, Gordon and the gimps back in Canary Wharf. The only difference was that this time, we were all honest with each other. We genuinely wanted to know what was going on. It wasn't easy, as I discovered our bonus systems was designed to be opaque. It was part-cash, part-equity stake, and nebulous. But some truths emerged. We compared our payments with the figures Gary and some of the boys had bragged about, taking off a small percentage to come up with the likely true figure. We had a bit of information from the secretaries as well. And if the numbers were true, it appeared as if the girls in the company had been shafted compared to the guys.

What could we do? There appeared to be an entirely different pay scale for men and women's bonuses. But ultimately, bonus payments are entirely discretionary. Amounts allocated to different employees can be easily explained by anything, such as, 'he added value here', 'he was instrumental in winning new business there', etc. It's a dilemma for women and endemic throughout the industry. City girls know all too well that the women who collect cheques in court rarely collect cheques in the City again. And despite everything, I wasn't ready to give it up just yet.

Part of me hoped that my pathetic bonus might bring Alex and I back together. If he didn't want a high-flying wife, per se, then he should be pleased I'd been brought back down to earth so sharply. As it turned out, I got barely more than a shrug when I passed on my news. He was staring at the Bloomberg data when I began telling him about my bonus and his eyes kept flashing back to it as I explained what I thought everyone else had been paid. He paused momentarily, then gave the monitor his full attention again straight afterwards. I went crazy. 'What is going on with us? Why aren't we talking any more? Why don't we care what's happening to each other?'

Alex finally engaged with me. It's ironic, bearing in mind the fact that I'd left that world behind, but when we fought that night we fought like traders: shouting and screaming across the room, both desperate to win every argument and score as many points as we could. In the weeks ahead, I'm ashamed to say that we would fight like City bankers: dirty, twisting the rules, changing the story and being as underhand as we dared. But however we rowed it was, of course, a zero-sum game, just like work. There are no winners or losers when two people realise they married far too soon and far too fast and far too young. There's no year-end bonus to be the first or the last to admit that five months is a crazily short courtship. And there's no trend pattern to follow as you seek out your next move.

We rode out the storms for many more months. We had moments when we almost connected again. But our outwardly perfect marriage was like an overvalued stock, and the only way to go was down. There were more moments when we were very far apart. And when the end came, it was triggered by something utterly silly and surreal.

For reasons I will never understand, my engagement ring had become a huge bone of contention between us. I often took it off to protect it at home – who doesn't? Sometimes I'd take it off to avoid unwanted attention from thieves, or for meetings or presentations at work. Plenty of City Girls have to do that if they want to be taken seriously. It was bad enough being patronised as a favoured daughter by some of our older clients. I couldn't bear them thinking I was a trophy wife with a rich husband as well. Alex began to monitor when I did and didn't wear the damn thing. It felt as if he took notes. Could he have created a special spreadsheet? Graphs?

'If you want to be in this marriage then you wear my ring every day. If you don't, then we'll end it,' he said one evening when I took the ring off to load the dishwasher and clean up around the kitchen.

'What are you talking about?'

'You're not wearing your ring.'

'I'm doing the housework.'

'That isn't the point. Wear it every day or I'll take it back.'

I argued the point a little longer. It's a piece of metal and a rock! Why does it mean so much? But as the cold weeks passed, so too did the comments. So one day I snapped. If Alex wanted symbolism then I'd give him symbolism with knobs on.

I worked the morning as normal and I left the office saying I was having a late lunch. Then I got a cab to Hatton Garden near Chancery Lane. 'Shopping for an engagement ring, love?' the cabbie asked with a big smile as he pulled up in the middle of the street, diamond stores ahead, and diamond stores behind.

'No. I'm selling one,' I said, with a lump in my throat.

I picked my dealer almost at random. The store closest appeared to be empty so I walked in. 'It's a nice ring,' the jeweller admitted cautiously. 'It's a *very* nice ring,' I said icily. No way was he ripping me off. 'It's 2.34 carats and the colour is D,' I said, echoing Alex's wedding day words from what felt like a lifetime ago, when we'd been happy. A flash of respect edged into the appraiser's eyes, which made me both pleased and angry.

The dealer offered me £7,500. It was more than he'd have given a dumb blonde, of course, but less, far less, than the stone was really worth. I took the money and left the store without saying another word.

I headed back to work, convinced that everyone in the office would be able to tell I'd done something irrevocable and terrible. No one could, of course. I left at 5 p.m. exactly and hurried home. I packed my clothes and possessions, ordered a taxi and headed to a hotel. I needed to find a new flat and start a new life. Alex and I had had several difficult conversations, but neither of us had any fight left in us. We would get a divorce. We wouldn't even talk about blame. And I wasn't going to take a penny from him. I'd banked the symbolic £7,500 from the sale of the blasted ring. That would be the end of it.

'Take things slowly, but try to smile and have some fun again,' my friend Katrina said, trying to comfort me in my isolation. Fun? In the derivatives business? In Mayfair in a very grim 2009? It certainly wasn't going to be easy. But you know what? I decided I might as well try.

As for me, I was left wondering where all the really handsome City boys had gone. I wasn't planning to date anyone again for the next decade or so, but a bit of eye candy would be welcome.

So how else could I shake up my suffocating office? Something very out of character occurred to me when I read the latest memo from our main boss. He didn't have a computer so he dictated his messages to his secretary or wrote them out longhand. She then typed them up and distributed them by email. His language was so old-fashioned and florid that I could almost hear a quill pen scratch over parchment when I read it. It was just waiting to be spoofed – so that's what I did.

I wrote out a typically long-winded memo about the one subject that brought our whole office together: tea breaks. We had immaculate kitchen areas and real china crockery in the building and the most civilised part of the day was making a cuppa. My joke memo said that all these facilities were being removed to save money amidst the economic down turn. I pressed send just before close of business on March 31st. The memo was in everyone's in-box on April Fool's Day.

Amazingly enough no one got the joke. In fact it was pandemonium when I arrived the next morning. It was worse than the days Merrill, AIG and HBOS hit the rocks and Lehman Brothers went bust. 'What do you think will be cut next? Will it be our jobs?' I was asked before I'd even got to my desk. 'Can they really do this? Is it legal to remove the tea?' someone else was asking.

It went on for ages. Then the crisis travelled. Our

regional offices were sent the memo, and we had panic calls from some of them. What have I done? I kept thinking. What's worse than an April Fool's joke that falls flat? One that totally succeeds. It was when they left a message for our boss, on a golfing holiday in California, that I began to panic myself. I had a horrible feeling he might charter a plane and fly back to Britain to man the barricades. I looked guiltily towards the fire exit. If he did, then I'd better scarper fast.

Someone, somewhere, worked out that it might have been a joke at about 10 a.m. But no one laughed. All everyone wanted to do was find the culprit. Once more, my eyes were on the door.

'Was it you, Suzana?' I was asked the following day by one of the IT girls.

'No,' I said, crossing my fingers under my desk.

'We know it was you,' she said. Oops.

'April Fool's?' I offered, weakly.

As it turned out I wasn't just forgiven I was applauded. I know it was a bit unprofessional, but tea-gate became a little office legend. Certainly it was no worse than the paper airplanes and inflatable sex dolls thrown around trading floors when those guys were having some down time. As the markets froze and business collapsed we were suddenly facing a strange new office enemy in Mayfair: boredom. Instead of the blood thumping panic of getting enough done during trading hours some colleagues quite literally had nothing to do for hours at a stretch. With no new clients to service we resorted to surfing the web and trying to look busy.

So a little light relief didn't go amiss. I thought of Jason in my first job. He'd made my life bearable back then, so maybe this had been my turn to do the same here. My aim had been to try and make people smile, to actually make someone laugh. It wasn't easy.

I decided to leave the company the following week. A year or so earlier, I had escaped Canary Wharf with what felt like one of the last job offers in town. Lightning struck twice. I bombarded head-hunters with my CV. The catty guy who had told me bankers were extinct wasn't answering his phone. The recruitment firm that led me to Mayfair appeared to have gone bust by this point. But personal contacts and recommendations could still conjure up new opportunities so I put the word out and somehow managed to get made an extraordinary offer.

# Chapter 17

I TOOK THE CALL at my desk. It was a confident, deep voice. I put the caller's age at about fifty and his net-worth at about £4 million, even in the slump. Sometimes you can just tell. He asked for me by name and told me where he was calling from. These guys aren't clients, I thought. My heart was already racing. This was how the game was played. 'Perhaps you would like to meet?' he suggested. 'Perhaps we could help one another.'

I could barely stop smiling for the rest of the day. It wasn't so much the potential escape route that excited me, but the fact that I'd been noticed. Someone has spotted what I can do! I looked around the office, all the rich, thick carpets and rich, not so thick, colleagues. I'd miss some of the women – particularly Lauren and Heather. But I wouldn't miss the incomprehensible bonus system, or my gruesome client meetings. Everyone had always said that the only way to survive the City was to stay constantly on the move. I was ready.

My contact had suggested a restaurant in Notting Hill for the interview. We would meet after work for an early evening dinner. For all the jokes about fake dental appointments, you do have to be a little discreet about job hunting and poaching.

I met him at the table. He looked exactly the way I had guessed he would. Perhaps early- to mid-fifties, thin grey pinstripes, salt-and-pepper hair and hungry eyes behind expensive glasses. I was wearing a camel Patrizia Pepe suit and had my hair tied back. It was a relaxed but expensive restaurant. But this was still business.

Interest rates around the world had been cut pretty much as far as they could go. The global economy needed a global rescue package. Markets were still inscrutable. Investment banks around the world continued to be bailed out by the government, or more controversially, left to fail. We had plenty to talk about over pre-dinner drinks.

'So, you're not entirely happy in your current position?' That was exactly what I had wanted him to say. You can't be seen to be too disloyal too early in these types of discussions. I tried to sow a few innocuous seeds of doubt without criticising the firm too specifically. 'And your personal life? I gather you have had some upheavals there as well?' His eyes flashed to my unadorned left hand, and the restaurant started to spin just a little. There are things you cannot ask in job interviews, especially of women. There are subjects that are legally off-limits, most notably a candidate's marital status, or intention to become a mother. 'You're single, I gather,' my companion continued. I noticed he had drunk far more of our rich red wine than I. 'But you're far too pretty to be single. I think something should be done about that.' His chair felt closer now than it had before. I realised that nothing about this meeting was business at all. It was personal.

He carried on talking as our sea bass arrived. It appeared that he hadn't had any upheavals in his home life. But not through want of trying. Thankfully he spared me the exact 'my wife doesn't understand me' cliché. But that was the basic premise. Though why he believed that I, at twenty years his junior, might understand him better, was beyond my comprehension.

Our main course plates had been taken away and I'd declined a dessert but been unable to refuse a coffee. 'I've got a room in a hotel over on Portobello Road. It's a suite. The one where Kate Moss and Johnny Depp had their champagne bath. Don't you think that sounds like a lot of fun?'

Suzana, don't throw your wine in his face. Don't make him think he's worth it. I finished my drink and managed to smile sweetly. 'I'll just pop to the Ladies first,' I said. Then I left the restaurant without saying goodbye. I'd love to know how long he stayed.


I probably shouldn't have expected much from a hedge fund manager, to be honest. Those guys aren't exactly renowned for treating women as equals. Someone once gave a statistic that only seven in a hundred employees in the hedge fund industry are female. At the most senior levels, this figure falls to just one in a hundred. Indeed, there are probably more female astronauts and Michelin-starred chefs than there are top hedge fund managers. And this could be one explanation behind their precipitous downfall in the 2008–2009 financial crisis. A brief look back in history shows men have committed most of the securities frauds, Ponzi schemes and corporate scandals. Moreover, evidence shows that organisations run by secret male societies are screwed up – just look at Long Term Capital's cowboys, al-Qaeda, or the Bush Administration.

Hedge funds had always been portrayed as the enemy when I was trading in Canary Wharf. They were the source behind the market manipulation and insider trading that thwarted our time-honoured trading strategies. Market manipulation can be described as a deliberate attempt to interfere with the free and fair operation of the market to create artificial, false or misleading appearances with respect to the price of, or market for, a security, commodity or currency.

Their tactics made our lives miserable and contributed significantly to the increasing volatility of the markets. I encountered most of the fund managers in Mayfair, where many funds are based. They were split between young, ambitious men in their dress-down chinos and the older, self-regarding ex-investment bankers who had the contacts and skills to survive within such a cut-throat new industry. 'Why can't the regulators exercise some degree of control, at least for the massive-sized funds?' I'd asked Charlie when we'd talked about the issue back in the early days.

'Hedge fund managers are a secretive bunch,' he admitted. When it comes to where they're investing, how much they're making, or how many women they're dating, mum is the word. Hedge funds accelerated their assault on markets after the 2001 market downturn, when investors sought ways to profit in both bull and bear markets ("long" or "short" strategies.) In other words, they would generate absolute returns betting on the deterioration of companies in downturns, getting their "Alpha" while most of the market got nada. Conventional "long-only" funds, such as pension funds, can't short equities. So investors have poured cash into these opportunistic vehicles in the past decade or so, and investment banks set up their own "in-house" hedge funds, thus proliferating these cowboys' bonanzas. Larger banks had the advantage of having access to information on share splits from their mergers and acquisitions departments, or the equity research from their research departments. There is a supposed "Chinese wall" that exists within all investment banks to prevent this: an internal "wall" between two departments which is meant to ensure that conflicts of interest don't arise. For instance, a bank might have a Corporate Finance department that advises on takeovers and mergers, and a Portfolio Management division that invests client money in shares. If the fund managers were to overhear the M&A guys in the canteen discussing an impending deal, that would be insider dealing. Chinese walls, enforced by a bank's Compliance department, are meant to ensure that the corporate financiers don't talk to the hedge fund managers about their work. But for some reason, this sensitive information has a way of diffusing through this "wall" with such effortless inertia, it's what you might call "financial market osmosis",' Charlie finished.

The next man to take me to a restaurant was honourable. It was for a seven-thirty breakfast meeting and you can't get less sexually charged than that. We were at a French restaurant on the edge of the City and he really did want to talk business. He ran a boutique derivatives trading consultancy in the West End. Better still, he had a vacancy.

I signed a new contract in his office later that week and headed back to Mayfair to resign. My manager made the briefest of efforts to change my mind, but I could hardly have missed the look of relief that flooded over his face when I gave him the news. Heads were going to roll, eventually, and it must have made his day when someone like myself left of their own accord. I gave the news to Lauren, Heather, Gary, some of the guys, and made a graceful exit. No one was in the mood for leaving drinks by that point. Over the past few years, everyone got tired of the forced camaraderie of those painful events.

# Chapter 18

I WORE AN UPDATED VERSION of my trusty Armani suit when I began what would be my fifth job in little more than four years. As usual, I was nervous on my first day. Maybe you never lose that feeling, however many jobs you start. But two weeks into it, I was feeling totally at home. My new bosses ran a tight ship. They hadn't over-stretched in the boom years, so they weren't suffering too badly in the crunch. 'We're small, but perfectly formed,' the senior partner had said with a grin over that first breakfast. He was right.

The company was based in a gorgeous Georgian building in the heart of the West End. But unlike my previous Mayfair office this interior was as modern as anything in Canary Wharf. We had some gorgeous, minimalist art in our entrance hall, sleek white desks in the main office and a good atmosphere throughout the firm. I had a tough but clearly defined role in the derivatives trading team and I loved it. I could meet my targets by working feverishly hard for sustained periods, then sit back and consider new market strategies when it was slightly quieter. All in all it was the perfect City combination – a world away from the screaming madness of intraday trading in the Wharf.

Within a month, I'd started to make friends. Over a few quick coffees and lunches a few of us swapped stories about the ups and downs of all our previous jobs. I told my story of tea-gate, and promised not to do anything similar to them if we were all still there next April Fool's Day. Over drinks one night I even found myself opening up and telling a couple of my new colleagues about my marriage and my divorce. I'd probably only seen Alex two or three times since leaving our old home. I knew from the City grapevine that he was still hanging on in there in Canary Wharf. I had no idea if he was seeing anyone else. But if he was, I'd have bet a lot of money that she wasn't a fellow trader.

'If you fancy going on a date I know a broker who's single and worth about £15 million,' one colleague said, bringing me sharply out of my reverie. 'If I wasn't married myself I'd consider him.' She was a fiercely intelligent French girl named Laetitia and one of the most stylish women I'd ever seen in the City. I looked across at her and smiled. 'I've only really been on a couple of dates since Alex,' I said. 'They were both City Boys, and they were both disasters because as usual all they talked about was money. If this guy gives it all up and becomes something creative like a painter then let me know. But if he's stuck in the City, I think I'm going to pass.'

Despite turning Laetitia's offer down, dating City Boys was pretty much our sole topic of conversation for the rest of that night. We categorised different types of colleague as if they were investments. My favourite was Mr Predictable, the relationship equivalent of gold. 'He's only desirable in times of war, invasion, major economic uncertainty or if we get terribly fat,' said my other colleague Lorraine. She was one of the team secretaries and a fabulous source of office gossip. When we tried to find an investment equivalent of Mr Married she had plenty of theories of who in our office might be playing away. 'Always remember that there are no secrets from me,' Lorraine said.

When we left the restaurant on Regent Street we all kissed goodbye and I walked west to my flat in Marylebone. It had been a lovely evening but I had felt a little worried towards the end. I wasn't having an affair but I did have a secret. And I desperately wanted to keep it.

It had begun with an uneventful Tube ride. I had nothing to read for once, and had been flicking through the free newspapers on the Tube just before leaving my old firm. It appeared that *thelondonpaper* was looking for a new columnist to replace Geraint Anderson, the trader whose weekly exposés of banking excess had just been transformed into the bestselling book *City Boy*. A new financial insider was required to carry on his good work. Could it be me? I'd never done much writing before. But I did like a challenge. I thought about it all the way home and toyed with the idea for the rest of the night. I certainly wouldn't be short on material if I took over Geraint's City beat. I'd long since believed that the whole credit crunch could have been avoided if there were more women in the City. An anonymous newspaper column would be the perfect place to express those thoughts.

I emailed a poem to the paper's editor the following day: *Prettier than your secretary, Smarter than your boss, Pressed against you in the Tube, Enticing heels and gloss. You break a sweat, I'm in Chanel, Wait till you see my P&L. Not fulfilling any quotas, My credentials beyond compare, I am the new City player.*

He'll laugh and I won't ever hear a word, I thought. But two days later I had a reply. The editor, Stefano Hatfield, liked my poem and wanted me to write two or three sample columns of 400 or so words each. Then he invited me to lunch at Shoreditch House in the East End. It was full of media types and quite cool – a total change from any City haunt I'd frequented. No one was wearing ties, pinstripes looked to be banned and the women all looked like models. I adored it. Stefano was really encouraging and two weeks later 'City Girl' was born. A sexy silhouette would run across the top of my column every Monday. I could finally relate the female side of the City. I could write on anything I thought was relevant. But I had to keep my true identity under wraps. Being undercover was a thrill. I felt like a spy sometimes, writing my stories at night or at the weekend and trying to make sure that neither Lorraine nor anyone else in my new office could recognise me from the scenarios I described.

Not everyone has approved of everything I've written and you can't hide from your opinions or predictions when every past column can be read online. But I've loved shaking things up in the column. I've certainly never had an empty email in-box the day after publication. And as the credit crunch drags on and as ever more financial fraudsters creep out from under their filthy rocks, there's been no shortage of material to write about. Commentating on the City made me feel even better about having finally broken into it four years ago.

That's one of the reasons why I started going to my City women networking events again. I'd been thinking about those girls for a while. I wanted to see if the old banking queens were still fighting their corners. They were. There were fewer of them, perhaps. But they were as feisty as ever and they always had new perspectives on the challenges the City was facing. The speakers we had at the meetings never shied away from the issues of the day. We all talked about what had gone wrong with the City and why. We considered who could be put right and how. I never once left a meeting without feeling positive about the future. I was fired up about what City Girls could achieve when they got together – which was why I kept trying to persuade every other City Girl I met to attend.

*     *     *

Top of my list were Lauren and Heather. The three of us had stayed in touch and we got together about two months after I'd switched jobs. We'd picked our favourite Shepherd's Market bar and we were wildly impressed by its latest recruit: a blond and handsome Polish waiter. 'It's not as if the men don't spend all day ogling us,' Heather said when we realised what we were doing. 'Don't let's feel guilty. It's payback time.'

We were all in great moods that night, ironically. The global economy was still tanking – in some ways, it was actually getting worse. The markets were tougher and more defiant than ever. But we were all feeling remarkably good, as Lauren and Heather reckoned they had proof that we were all going to make it. They told me Marcus had been off ill for the past two weeks – rumour said he had gout. So with him out of the picture Heather had gone on a client meeting with one of the other female executives. 'Suzana, it was like a dream. When there's one girl in the boardroom they're pissed off at you. When there's two they get used to it. One of the old boys we were presenting to even got up and poured the tea. It was brilliant.'

I didn't let them in on my gig as *thelondonpaper*'s City Girl, but I started talking about the specifics I wrote about, how the boys had broken the City and how it was time for us girls to fix it. They agreed. Everyone still hated bankers in the summer of 2009. But for the first time in ages, I was proud of working in the City. It had cost me my marriage and been more stressful than I'd ever imagined. But it was still the

most immensely exciting place in the world to work –
and that night, the three of us agreed it could only get
better.

'Women are taking over in medicine and the law,'
Lauren said as we shared our shot of girl power. 'The
City is the final frontier. But if we don't get into
the top positions now we never will. This will be the
moment we prove we can beat the boys at their own
game.' For the rest of the night, we toasted a future
where there would be more than two girls in every
twenty-strong intake of gimps. Heather joked about a
city where nail bars might spring up in place of some
of the lap dancing bars. But deep down all three of us
knew that the City's problems were about far more
than just the battle of the sexes. The issue wasn't that
there are so many men and so few women. It's that
there are so many people of both sexes who don't see
the full picture. The traders I'd worked with in Canary
Wharf might well have known everything about the
market. But they barely knew a thing about their own
firm. They certainly didn't know how many eagle-eyed
staffers were slogging away in the darkness of the back
offices. They didn't know that those colleagues collated
huge amounts of information and would readily share
it to anyone who bothered to ask. Working in isolation is the first big curse of the City. That's how all
the rogue traders from Nick Leeson in Singapore to
Jérôme Kerviel in Paris got away with it for so long.
It's crazy that the City allows people to stay so cut off
from their peers. It's like having doctors who are only

taught about arms and don't know who to call if they've got a question about hands.

'You should come to my next networking event,' I said suddenly as we ordered some nibbles from the bar. 'It's a special one, at a hotel right by the Bank of England. There are some great speakers then there's a wine tasting session in the hotel dining room with some professional sommeliers.'

Lauren and Heather both rolled their eyes. 'I don't like the thought of it being an extension of the office. I don't think I handle any more talk about derivatives after hours,' said Lauren. I waved the thought away.

'I promise that no one will ask you to deconstruct a swap. Look, if you hate it I'll buy you both cocktails in Corney and Barrow to make up for it. I'm serious that the more people we all meet the better we're going to do. Will you come?'

I managed to persuade them by the end of the night – and when the event itself came round it was a total success. Whistleblowers, self-regulation and best practice were just three of the topics under discussion. No surprise to learn that most of the whistleblowers came from the lower ranks of the business. They tend to be the people who check the numbers add up. They're the grafters who are normally heard far too late, the people who see everything because no one is ever looking at them. When you look at vast scams like Enron in America you also realise that an awful lot of whistleblowers are women. These are the City Girls the regulators should be listening to – and even recruiting if we're ever to get out of the mess we're in.

I lost sight of both Lauren and Heather as everyone mingled towards the end of the night. I'd been talking to a younger girl who reckoned her current job was too dull and too far from the real action. Everything she said seemed horribly familiar. 'If I don't move soon I'll miss my chance,' she said at one point. Did I manage to persuade her that she'd end up a stronger front office candidate if she paid her dues and stayed where she was for a bit longer? Probably not. But I think it's the truth and I surprised myself by saying it. I wished, somehow, that I hadn't always been in such a hurry myself. For if isolation is the first curse of the City, then the ridiculously high staff turnaround is the second. The obsession with recruiting fresh blood from outside, the refusal to bring down internal barriers or seriously consider internal candidates weakened every organisation. It produced skill and knowledge vacuums in even the best firms. It set our business apart from almost any other industry in the world. No wonder it was hit so hard when the bad times finally came.

The Royal Exchange was bathed in glorious golden floodlights as I walked up Threadneedle Street hoping to find a taxi. I looked over towards the Stock Exchange and the Bank of England. I was right at the heart of the City – and perhaps for the very first time I felt completely at home. Sure, it had been a hell of a fight to get in. Sure, I'd had some terrible times when I'd been too stressed to think straight. I'd seen too little of my friends and I'd sometimes lost sight of the true value of money. I'd met and lost the man of my dreams in what felt like the blink of an eye. But I'd do it all again in an instant. I'd been lucky enough to see the tail end of the boom years. I'd slogged my way though the very worst days of the slump. Now I was ready for the City's next chapter. It would re-invent itself to spring back from the credit crunch. If the right decisions were made it would come back better and stronger. That was the City I wanted to be part of.

# Acknowledgements

I WANT TO THANK first and foremost all my ex-colleagues, ex-boyfriends, ex-husbands and ex-employers from the City. This book wouldn't have been possible without you.

Big thanks to everyone at *thelondonpaper* (Stefano Hatfield, Eva Simpson, Bridget Harrison and Dominic Midgley) for giving me the opportunity to write my 'City Girl' column. To my agent Andrew Lownie and my editor Louisa Joyner for their assistance.

Thanks to Sarah Western Balzer and Vic Daniels at www.hereisthecitynews.com, for their support of my column, and also to Michael Shnayerson at *Vanity Fair* for his encouragement and assistance with my writing. Also, thanks to Paul Samuel and Franklin Price for their assistance, because I always seem to get myself into trouble.

Thanks to my web designer Sophie Lodge, and the talented Drew Gardner.

To Matthew and Lynda Pudney, my surrogate parents in a foreign country. And to all my family and friends, for their continued support throughout my life.